Donald J. Trump and China

Donald J. Trump and China

John Franklin Copper

Hamilton Books

Lanham • Boulder • New York • Toronto • London

Published by Hamilton Books
An imprint of The Rowman & Littlefield Publishing Group, Inc.
4501 Forbes Boulevard, Suite 200, Lanham, Maryland 20706
Hamilton Books Acquisitions Department (301) 459-3366

6 Tinworth Street, London SE11 5AL

Copyright © 2019 by The Rowman & Littlefield Publishing Group, Inc.

All rights reserved. No part of this book may be produced in any form or by any electronic means, including information storage and retrieval systems,without written permission from the publisher, except by a reviewer who may quote passages in a review.

British Library Cataloguing in Publication Information Available

Library of Congress Control Number Available

ISBN 9780761871187 (pbk. : alk. paper)
ISBN 9780761871194 (electronic)

∞™ The paper used in this publication meets the minimum requirements of American National Standard for Information Sciences Permanence of Paper for Printed Library Materials, ANSI/NISO Z39.48-1992.

Contents

Preface vii

Acknowledgment xi

1 President Donald Trump's Upbringing, Thoughts, and His Understanding of China 1

2 President Obama's China Policy Legacy 7

3 Has President Obama Driven (bird caged) President-elect Trump into a Conflict with China? 15

4 Why China Likes Donald Trump: History Tells Us Something 19

5 President Trump's Decision to Honor the One-China Policy: How Best to Explain It? 23

6 The Challenge of China's Role as the World's Builder 29

7 The First Trump-Xi Meeting: Success or Failure? 33

8 Has President Trump's Worldview Become More Discernible? 37

9 Does the United States Expect Too Much of China in Dealing with North Korea? 41

10 Opponents and Supporters of China's One Belt One Road Project 47

11 President Trump Dismisses Steve Bannon: The China Policy Factor 51

12 The U.S. Liberal Media's Treatment of President Trump's Asia Trip Versus Asian Reporting 57

13 Explaining the Recent Tension in United States-China Relations 63

14 The U.S. Trade Deficit with China: Facing Dilemmas 69

15 The Worsening U.S. Trade Deficit with China: Heading for a Trade War? 75

16 The Top Two Targets of Western Liberal Media Bias: President Donald Trump and China 79

17 Avoiding a United States-China Trade War: Understanding Donald Trump May Help 87

18 Will the Western Media Prod America and China into a War? 91

19 Understanding the United States-China Impasse on North Korea 95

20 Will President Trump Ignite a War with China? 99

21 China's Rise as an Innovative Country 105

22 Why the United States is Losing (has lost?) the Number One World Power Ranking to China 111

23 Will China Meddle in America's Mid-term Election? 117

24 Does President Donald Trump Dislike China and Chinese? On the Contrary! 121

25 Dealing with the U.S. Trade Deficit with China 125

26 China Robs U.S. Intellectual Property and Technology: How True? How Big? How to Fix It? 131

27 America and China: Long-Term Friends or Enemies? 137

Index 143

About the Author 151

Preface

Years before he was elected president of the United States in November 2016, when he thought about and wrote about United States foreign policy Donald J. Trump proclaimed America's biggest problem was China. Furthermore, it was a problem not being solved. And it was the fault of U.S. leaders for allowing the trade deficit—the leading problem with China—to reach monumental proportions and his country to be hurt by it.

Trump wrote about China in several of his books. From reading what he wrote it was easily discernable that he had great respect for China. He demonstrated that in real life: He encouraged his grandchildren to learn Chinese and speak it daily. They did. Later they even entertained President Xi and the first lady and other of China's top leaders in Chinese. On once occasion the event was on national T.V. in China. It went viral with the Chinese people. They and Chinese leaders felt President Trump was special.

It was also apparent that Donald Trump not only respected China; he understood the rise of China and its importance to the United States—more than any other country, including Russia or Japan, or even any group of countries, including the European Union. China was growing faster economically and was putting larger amounts of money into science and technology and the military. That and more were making a difference.

Donald likewise grasped the reality that China was a challenge to the United States—America's foremost one. That was reflected in the huge U.S. trade deficit with China, which he knew was unsustainable because it caused the shuttering of many American factories and the loss of jobs to U.S. workers. Not only that, it accounted in large measure for the massive debt the United States had accumulated, which had become a threat to the United States and to the global financial system.

The way to fix this was to negotiate. And as president that is what he did. He made friends with China's leaders. He made it plain to them what he wanted. Chinese officials understood how to negotiate; and they did.

The road was not an easy or smooth one. China pledged to help fix the U.S. trade deficit by buying more American products. China did; but owing to the much-improved U.S. economy under President Trump

America bought even more from China. Thus the trade deficit grew bigger rather than shrinking.

China's leaders also promised to help President Trump deal with North Korea's Kim Jong Un; his nuclear weapons and missile tests threatened South Korea, Japan and even the U.S. China's leaders regarded it as a serious unwanted problem and so acted. However, they were cautious: They did not want the North Korean regime to implode as that might put U.S. troops in South Korea close to the Chinese border. There was a record in history of that.

China wanted to move slowly on the two issues—trade and North Korea. Helping fix the U.S. trade deficit was necessary but it would cause unemployment in China, which might cause social unrest. North Korea was a difficult issue; China was on the U.S. side, but its leaders were cautious and wanted to move slowly. Also some Chinese leaders opined that U.S. presidents had been weak on dealing with these issues for years; why would Donald Trump be any different?

Tensions between Trump's America and China followed. There were serious issues separating them—not only the trade deficit and North Korea but also intellectual property and technology losses the United States suffered, differences over the South China Sea, Taiwan and more. China and the United States were competing global powers—the only real world powers.

Conflict was to be expected between the two preeminent world powers. China was determined to rise; it has been down too long. It possessed the ingredients of a big power, if not the biggest. Chinese leaders nurtured nationalism and patriotism to help them realize China's destiny. Trump wanted to make America great again. Like Chinese leaders he also said he was a nationalist.

It soon became obvious the liberal Western media espoused extreme enmity toward China as well as Donald Trump because China threatened the liberal world order. They did not want cordial or even peaceful relations between the two.

President Trump working with President Xi did. He said working with China is a *sin qua non* to maintain world peace, a stable global financial system, keeping the lid on nuclear proliferation, dealing with global environmental problems, containing terrorism and much more. Their working relationship was an indispensible one for both and for the world.

Following are essays I have written and published online on President Trump dealing with China and China's leaders. It is hoped that they will enlighten the reader about the president's commitment to interacting successfully with China, how he can and will do that, and how important it is.

The essays are generally in chronological order, reflecting President Trump's view of China and his China policy that were both a departure from U.S. stances toward China taken by previous presidents and how the relationship evolved for him and for Chinese leaders. Some ideas and topics are repeated from a different time perspective given political, economic and other changes in the U.S., China and international politics.

Acknowledgment

The articles herein were originally published by IPPReview online. The author wishes to thank IPPReview for allowing them to be used here.

ONE

President Donald Trump's Upbringing, Thoughts, and His Understanding of China

When Donald J. Trump entered the presidential race and even more so after he became America's 45th president in January 2017, his antagonists, the U.S. media, Hollywood, academe and the Democratic Party, denigrated him, his background, his knowledge and his policies.

The narrative was hypercritical when the discussion turned to U.S. foreign policy. Articles in the *New York Times,* the *Washington Post* and other liberal mainstream media outlets described Trump as having no upbringing that would help him understand diplomatic protocol or the established tenets of past and present foreign policy. He was said to be an unthinking protectionist, isolationist, and anti-globalist. Donald Trump, they posited, would wreck the global order.

Regarding specifically U.S. relations with China, they said, Trump was even worse. His charges that China was a currency manipulator, that China was the source of Americans losing their jobs and the shuttering of U.S. factories and that a 45 percent tariff should be applied to China's imports to the United States were said to be provocative in the extreme and dangerous. Trump's opponents even said he would start a trade war.

But the refrain that Trump lacked experience to deal with China (and foreign affairs generally) was not heard so much after it was learned that Trump had conferred at length with Henry Kissinger, that one of his favorite books was Sun Tzu's *The Art of War,* that Trump had written about China (in his book *Time to Get Tough)* and that he had had significant business deals with the Chinese (including Chinese partners in building Trump Place in New York and Chinese investors in 1290 Avenue of the Americas and the Bank of American Building in San Francisco).

The question then arose: What did Trump think about China? In his book *Time to Get Tough* Donald Trump wrote: "China is our enemy" (for which Trump's detractors proffered the view that Trump would start a war with China). But Trump also said China was an enemy because of weak and incompetent government officials in the United States that were taken to the cleaners by smart, seasoned Chinese negotiators, and he would fix that and turn China into a friend.

What were Trump's strategies for doing that? In his book *The Art of the Deal* Trump signaled he would be a transactional president. He would apply commonsense rules of doing business to formulating foreign policy and conducting foreign affairs.

"Negotiate, negotiate, negotiate" was the basis of Trump's approach. Other candidates for president did not take this approach. It was unconventional. It emphasized pragmatic diplomacy rather than a value-oriented approach. But Trump certainly knew how to do business and China understood that.

Trump's perception of international politics, it was soon grasped, was that of the realist . . . comporting with his business background, his talks with Kissinger and his reading of Sun Tzu and others. For Donald Trump power—economic power, political power, but especially military power—were the foundation stones of an effective foreign policy.

Trump's prime objective was to make the United States strong again. Doing this required reversing the American military's decline. This was typical realist thinking espoused by many of America's past presidents: Kennedy, Nixon and Reagan. It underscored the importance of security, U.S. national interests and hard power over soft power.

Trump was also a nationalist. Patriotism fit his psyche. Being born in the United States was a blessing to Donald. He loved his country. He was given boundless opportunities throughout his lifetime. He was successful in business and other pursuits. "America first" was thus a natural, and painfully needed, idea, to Trump.

Barack Obama's transnational, globalist presidency, in Trump's mind, had failed miserably. To Trump, disparaging America was not a good policy. Leading from behind was not leading at all. Absent America's headship the world was rudderless and worse off for that.

Donald Trump was also aware that the world was at a tipping point. The Pope spoke of a "world at war everywhere" and a blurred divide between war and peace. The U.S. National Intelligence Council had recently described the world as "dangerous." Richard Haass, president of the Council on Foreign Relations, in his new book *A World in Disarray,* wrote of the world being in a state of "decay, even collapse."

This was also Trump's view. Many of his advisors and friends agreed with him about this, convincing him that what he thought and said were true.

Trump's way or *modus operandi*, partly learned from his growing up in the world of business, but also acquired from seeing life's successes as often a matter of destroying and starting anew, was to discard the "out of date world system." Free trade wasn't working as too many countries were cheating. Security systems were failing, as many U.S. allies were not doing their share.

Donald Trump had another relevant personality trait. He did not fear chaos or messiness. As Newt Gingrich, former speaker of the House of Representatives, wrote of Trump in his book *Understanding Trump,* Donald emphasized speed in getting things done, not mistake avoidance.

One is reminded of one of former President Harry Truman's famous sayings: "What is worse than making a mistake is not making a decision." That was Trump! Gingrich even called this the "Trump Doctrine."

Trump also followed the dictum of knowing who is important and who isn't in any situation, but especially during critical negotiations.

On the world scene, Trump viewed China as having a special ranking in terms of its importance. He devoted an entire chapter on China in *Time to Get Tough* to this. China had become a formidable world power. No other country was accorded that status. Trump saw Europe, Russia, Japan, and other purported world powers as regional organizations or countries in demographic, economic and military decline.

Donald Trump also espoused deep respect for China's history and culture and its potential to influence the world in positive ways. His grandchildren were studying Chinese and speaking it daily. In this regard Trump was almost without peers among top U.S. politicians.

Thus, while criticizing China harshly during the campaign and even after he became president, he promptly arranged a "summit" meeting with President Xi Jinping at Trump's "second White House" in Mar-a-Lago, Florida.

Trump's way of thinking shone through at the meeting. He felt that to do government business, as in making commercial deals, one needed to meet with the top leader, look him or her in the eyes and get to know him or her. Hence Trump arranged a prolonged one-on-one meeting with President Xi with only an interpreter present. This built trust and understanding. It was something Trump considered invaluable.

Forthwith the two made important deals. President Xi agreed to buy U.S. beef and to allow U.S. financial companies to compete for business in China. Both were hugely important to fixing America's trade imbalance with China. In fact, they were big money items.

More was to come of their "100-days of negotiations" plan. Then the 100 days was extended. President Xi did what he promised. Trump's critics, though, carped that Xi didn't live up to the spirit of the deal. To

Trump Xi was indeed a tough dealer; he didn't give much more than he promised.

President Trump reciprocated. He sent a representative to President Xi's One Road One Belt opening forum in May and gave his blessing to the gargantuan project. President Obama had opposed it and tried to obstruct it. The Western media did not like it; it mirrored China's fast rise and it would undermine the Western, liberal world order. Several European nations expressed their opposition because it did not include human rights or governance in its agenda and they did not like China's preference for negotiating bilaterally rather than multilaterally. India and Japan (temporarily) were opposed as it encroached on their external influence.

President Trump realized he had important things in common with President Xi. Both were builders. Both felt this was essential to improving their countries. Both favored innovation and progress. Both were globalists and wanted to help the world become more modern and more prosperous.

At home both regarded bureaucracy and corruption enemies of efficient government. The two presidents saw they had to do things themselves and engage on many fronts to understand and then conquer obstacles in their own political systems.

On the foreign policy front they favored sovereignty. They reckoned that the nation-state was the indispensible actor in global affairs. If nations negotiated their differences well and engaged in astute transactions international politics would work.

Trump, as Xi, liked to deal with other countries one-on-one. He didn't like group diplomacy. Both perceived that groupthink international bureaucracies got in the way of getting things done.

Speaking of Donald Trump's character, he was brusque and often unnerving to both his friends and enemies. That was his nature. President Xi was calmer, but he also could be direct and candid. Other national leaders frequently said Xi was blunt and to the point.

Both Trump and Xi were whipping boys of the Western media. Trump because he opposed the political elite and criticized its symbiotic relationship with the press, Democrats and Hollywood. Xi because the Western mainstream media shuddered at the idea that China's rise would ultimately succeed and crowd out the Western, liberal world order.

Both Trump and Xi understood that the United States and China were competitors and that the nature of their relationship was to some degree an antagonistic one. That is the nature of things.

They would disagree. They would defend their views and their nation's interests. But they would also be friends and even allies. As Henry Paulson advised in his book *Dealing with China* (and President Trump respected his advice), in order to maintain a stable global financial and trade system, to contain nuclear proliferation, to combat terrorism, and much more, the United States and China had to work together as allies. President Trump took this advice to heart.

As a consequence, with Donald Trump president of the United States, United States-China relations gained a new high priority. Ties, Trump believed, would improve (when Trump assumed the high office they had not been worse than since before President Nixon) and would remain cordial and, most important, would work to the betterment of both countries and the world.

TWO

President Obama's China Policy Legacy

To understand President Trump's China policy it is instructive to examine what came before him or what he inherited.

What is called in the United States a president's "foreign policy legacy" usually refers to something he (or she in the future) has done or a policy or doctrine he initiated while in office that will have a lasting impact on America's relations with other countries and will be cited by future historians. Ordinarily it is something that is seen as positive, but that is not necessarily the case.

President Obama's legacy might have been his success in halting Iran from becoming a nuclear power. Or the U.S. pivot to Asia launched by Secretary of State Clinton in 2011 that Obama put into operation. However, both of these policy initiatives ran into difficulties and in retrospect did not generate the results hoped for. Even his supporters do not refer to them as "doctrines." Sometimes the president's Nobel Prize, his efforts to get the United States out of Middle East conflicts, and his opening relations with Cuba are cited; but they have faded in terms of the attention they once garnered and/or didn't rise to the level of a noteworthy legacy.

This brings us to what is considered President Obama's negative accomplishments. There are a number; but clearly the most poignant among them is the United States losing the status of the world's preeminent power to China. A number of scholars say that China's rise and its assuming the position of the world's most important, most powerful, most influential nation is something President Trump has or will cause. The trouble with this view is this already happened when President Obama was in office.

Considerable evidence can be mentioned, but most of what will be cited are trends or were events that had backgrounds or gestation periods before Obama became president. Nevertheless they are part of what was "bequeathed" to Donald Trump when he became president.

In 2009, the year Barack Obama became president, China outdid the United States in the value of output of its manufacturing sector. (The United States held that honor for a century, though China held it for around 1,800 years until 1840 when Great Britain became number one.) That same year China bested America in auto production (one of Americans' big claims to fame).

In 2010, China's Tianhe-1A was acclaimed in the global media the fastest computer in existence, replacing America's best. In 2011 China registered more patents than the United States. That year the length of China's express highways, put at 85,000 kilometers, surpassed the United States. Also, in 2011 China announced a program to send a man to the moon and establish a base there. (President Obama cancelled U.S. manned missions to the moon in 2010.)

In 2013, China became the largest trading country in the world, with its foreign commerce that year reaching nearly $4 trillion. It knocked the United States from that exalted position. China's tourists that year spent $129 billion around the world. Americans spent $86 billion and dropped behind China to second place in that realm. In 2014 China accounted for 60 percent of the world's skyscrapers completed in the past twelve months. China also became the foremost country in the world in express mail deliveries. Finally, the value of its e-commerce that year amounted to $323 billion. In all of these realms China bested the United States.

In 2015, China became the biggest market in the world for industrial robots (passing Japan and the United States). In 2016, China launched the World's first quantum satellite into orbit—allowing for absolutely secure communications. It was reported at the time that China was moving ahead of the United States in the space race with a probe planned to the far side of the moon and it likely replacing the International Space Station when it runs out of money in two years. Shortly after that China cut the ribbon on the world's largest radio telescope, edging out America's Arecibo Observatory that had that honor.

In 2016, President Obama's last year in office, Steven Chu, the former U.S. Secretary of Energy, noted that China has gotten ahead of America in everything from wind power to nuclear energy and was catching up in artificial intelligence, genetic engineering, 5-G broadband technology and the "Internet of things."

Chu also mentioned China has made "great leaps" in secret weaponry: a fifth generation stealth fighter (J-20), the aircraft carrier killer missile (DF-21D), an anti-ship cruise missile (YJ-12), a nuclear submarine (SSBN-094) and a long range intercontinental missile (DF-41-ICBM).

At this time China became the world's foremost nation for filing patents (more than a third of the world's total), new industrial design (50 percent compared to 9 percent for the United States) and trademarks (76 percent compared to 13 percent for the United States). This was explained in part by the fact China had 27 million students enrolled in colleges and universities (almost double the United States) and 40 percent were enrolled in science and technology courses (in contrast to a much smaller percent in the United States).

In addition to the above there are some other facts that truly astound. China was in the process of building a new Silk Road while adding a maritime belt—an endeavor known as the One Belt, One Road project that will connect Asia to Europe and Africa commercially and in other ways. Much of it was already on-line. Launched in 2013, when completed it will be the biggest such undertaking in human history at a cost of more than $1 trillion dollars. (By comparison the U.S. Marshall Plan to finance Europe's recovery after World War II, in current dollars, was just over $100 billion.)

Adding a bigger surprise to what most knew about China's economic prowess, data was published at this time on China's contribution to growth in the planetary product, or the world's GDP. China was accounting for almost thirty-nine percent of global expansion—four fold the United States and six fold the European Union. China, in other words, was the world's foremost growth engine by a huge margin in spite of somewhat smaller economy.

Related to this, China was plainly the driver behind poor and middle level nations prospering economically. China was providing more foreign aid and investment funds to promote their growth than the United States. In a number of countries China was providing billions of dollars while the United States helped with millions.

A side effect is the fact China had become the main force behind reducing global poverty. In 2015 the global media reported that China had been astonishingly successful at eliminating poverty in China to the tune of 450 to 600 million people (while poverty was on the increase in the United States) it was the world's leader in reducing penury globally. China almost alone made the United Nation's millennial global development goals succeed, the core one being cutting economic suffering around the world.

That same year it was reported that China's middle class (defined as having a net worth of between US$50,000 and $500,000) had grown to over one hundred million, was the largest in the world, and was still expanding very fast, while the middle class was shrinking in the United States. This was offered as evidence China's economy was well managed and America's wasn't. Some observers concluded that it was proof China's political system was more stable and that its leaders had the confidence of the populace, while the opposite was true in the United States under Obama and his predecessors (as witnessed in many public opinion polls on that topic). Also as a consequence China was now the favored model for developing countries for not only its economic but also its political system.

Paralleling China's rise to fame, the United States has revealed shocking evidence of a very rapid weakening in critical factors that relate to national power and global influence.

First is the matter of the U.S. economy and America's economic influence in the world. The 2008–09 global economic crisis, by the way triggered by the United States, uncovered financial policies and practices in the United States that were patently unsustainable. Thus the economic recession! But the crisis also exposed the fact that responses needed (and taken), only added to the burdens for Washington to keep its long dominant role in managing the world economy.

As a result monetary experts in other countries began to question the future of the dollar as *the* global currency. Historians then made comparisons with the devaluation of the British pound in the 1950s, after which the U.K. had to retreat from involvement in the Suez Crisis and then witnessed losing its status as an eminent world power. The question was: Would the United States' situation constitute history repeating itself?

In other words what happened in 2008–09 discredited America as a global financial leader and gave China an opportunity to play a much bigger role in managing international finance and all that went with that.

Looking at other data for the period leading up to the financial crisis (1998 to 2007) and what followed is similarly instructive. Before 2008 China's economy grew at an average rate of 9.95 percent; America's grew at a mean rate of 3.02 percent. In other words, China's economic growth was more than three times better. After the 2008–09 economic crisis China continued to grow fast while the United States fell into a period of protracted slow growth. By 2012 China's economy was more than fifty percent larger than it had been; America's had grown only a small fraction of that.

The biggest effects domestically of America's slow growth were a huge trade deficit, the loss of jobs and a gigantic debt owed to itself and to other countries, but most important in terms of global status money owed to China. The trade shortfall with China had existed for some years, almost since Beijing shifted to a free market economy under Deng Xiaoping, cut the size and authority of government, reduced taxes, and ended government planning and its harmful intervention in the economy. But the imbalance ballooned under President Obama. In 2009 it was under $227 billion. In 2015, the deficit was a record $366.7 billion.

This sent the U.S. debt owed to China to well over $1.2 trillion. Meanwhile the loss of jobs in the United States totaled 2.7 million and was still growing. Most of these losses were in manufacturing and affected every state in the United States. This, many Americans perceived, did profound and irreversible damage to their country. They were right. Clearly it fast diminished America's national power capabilities and undermined its influence throughout the world.

One cannot blame President Obama for all of this. Most of China's accomplishments in outdoing and it upstaging the United States were trends in progress before, some starting long before Obama entered the White House. The serious trade deficit with China began during the Clinton years. America falling behind in a number of the areas cited above was the consequence of horrendously expensive wars President George W. Bush launched after 9/11.

Anyway, there is more that can be mentioned about China's rise. The evidence grew exponentially as did its gravity throughout the Obama presidency. In other words, to use a term from nuclear physicists, they reached a critical mass under Obama.

The most important metric of change that reflected China's rise and America's fall and that arguable was in large measure attributable to President Obama's policies was that China would soon pass the United States in economic size—probably within five or ten years. Slow growth in the United States was the main reason (the slowest recovery after a recession in American history by a number of measures). Second, and related to the first, China would soon boast of a larger defense budget than the United States—expected by 2025 according to the Stockholm Internationl Peace Research Institute (owing to big cuts in U.S. defense spending resulting from the sequestration bill and China having maintained double-digit growth almost every year since 1991).

Certainly President Obama was responsible for deteriorating U.S.-China relations during his tenure in office, causing China's accomplishments to be seen more in terms of China defeating America in the course of pursuing its dream to become a world power rather than simply as a natural course of events.

In fact, relations with China were not as strained during any president's tenure since President Nixon engineered America's rapprochement with China in the late 1960s. Obama's falling out with China was reflected in his failed efforts to rescue the pivot to Asia policy and the Trans-Pacific Partnership deal that accompanied it late during his tenure as president. Both were anti-China and both had lost support at home and in Asia.

President Obama adopted policies and took actions to block China's rise in some maladroit ways while using tactics that seemed to reflect the view that the White House did not want to see China assist developing nations or make the world a better place to live. This made Obama look small and jealous.

In 2013 China announced founding the Asia Infrastructure Investment Bank (AIIB) and pledged $50 to $100 in initial funding. China's initiative was aimed at fixing the serious need in Asia for infrastructure. The Asian Development Bank estimated $8 trillion would be needed to fix it.) The

Obama administration immediately launched a rear-guard action to thwart China's plan by asking allies not to join. Obama feared the AIIB would undercut the Asian Development Bank, the World Bank and other institutions the United States had founded and largely controlled.

This effort failed as a host of countries joined the AIIB, including important U.S. allies—the U.K, Germany and some other European countries. By 2016 the number reached almost sixty countries. In August Canada signed on.

President Obama also opposed China's Yuan becoming a global currency. This failed and the International Monetary Fund blessed the Yuan to join four widely used currencies (the U.S. dollar, the Euro, the Pound and the Yen) to become one of the world's "elite" currencies. This decision was subsequently confirmed.

President Obama also took measures to obstruct China's one-belt, one road project (OBOR) mentioned above—also unsuccessfully. More than one hundred countries and international organizations signed on. It was projected OBOR will impact 70 percent of the world's population. China had 80,000 kilometers of high-speed railroad lines under construction (or finished) to make the project work.

President Obama even told the government of Thailand that the United States did not like China's proposal to build the Kra Canal across the narrow part of the peninsula in southern Thailand that would cut the shipping distance of goods going from the Middle East and South Asia to East Asia and which would be a boon to Thailand's development.

President Obama (in the context of the flagging TPP) said: "We cannot let countries like China write the rules of the global economy. We should write these rules."

Some Asian observers reacted by suggesting Obama had "resorted to military provocation, intervention and war" to halt China's global construction successes because his other efforts had failed. That seems to describe accurately Washington's less than popular efforts to base America's pivot to Asia more on military power than on economic might.

Shortly after this the Organization for Economic Development and Cooperation predicted China would very soon become the most powerful country in the world economically. According to a Pew Foundation poll, citizens of most Western European countries, including Germany, the U.K., France, and Russia, believed this had already happened. Ironically Americans believed this too. Other surveys done by Pew recorded more people on every continent believed China had become the world's superpower or soon will, passing the United States, than believed otherwise.

Explaining all of this, many observers noted that it comports with President Obama's "lead from behind" policy, his trans-nationalism, and his negative view of American exceptionalism. Some say this is what he wanted. In any case, Obama has, says his critics, overseen the historic transition in the international system from one dominated by America to one China was going to lead.

THREE

Has President Obama Driven (bird caged) President-elect Trump into a Conflict with China?

Some critics of the Obama administration charge that the president, in the final days of his administration, by ordering U.S. intelligence agencies to conduct a "full review" of Russian hacking of the U.S. election and then expelling Russian diplomats and closing down some of Moscow's "diplomatic" operations in the United States, deliberately sought to put his successor, Donald Trump, in an awkward cum vulnerable position in view of the latter's friendship with Russia.

In so doing Obama risked allowing President Putin the opportunity to undermine confidence in American democracy without proof that he affected the outcome of the election. President Obama's actions also seem to single out Russia when there were probably many hackers. Further, Obama's move came after he had conspicuously failed to act when Putin's Russia invaded the Crimea and later when Putin took control over the conflict in Syria.

Obama thus seemed to want to "set up" Trump. The media and Democrats accused Trump of collusion with Russia to win the election. Then came the Mueller investigation.

It also appeared that President Obama has implemented, or at least had not opposed or sought to block, legislation to birdcage President-elect Trump on future relations with China. In other words he has "arranged" obstacles for Trump to get along with Beijing.

President Obama's moves vis-à-vis China during the sunset days of his tenure in office, however, were of a different order than his Russian challenge. They are mainly efforts to get Congress to act and were of a legal (legislative) nature. This in some senses were worse than Obama's presidential orders against Russia as they could not be erased easily or ignored. In addition, there were funds allocated specifically to support them.

One is a new provision put into the U.S. National Defense Authorization Act that will allow U.S. military exercises with Taiwan and exchanges between high-ranking officers (flag officers). Visits were predicted to increase by 50 percent in 2017.

Then President Obama put his signature on the 2017 version of the Act just three weeks before the end of his term in office. He had heretofore not supported such a change in policy. Also his decision clearly did not comport with his China/Taiwan policy, notably concurring with Chinese leaders during his trip to China in 2009 that Taiwan was a Chinese "core interest" (which China would be willing to engage its military to protect) or with his subsequent moves to reduce America's commitments to Taiwan and perhaps even abandon the island.

President Obama's action clearly made Taiwan happy, though experts in Taipei said it was too little too late and may create serious dangers for Taiwan. No doubt it made Chinese leaders in Beijing uneasy cum angry and this came at a time when the Chinese military was said to be "anxious" about Taiwan.

In addition, it may have put President Trump at odds with Congress, where there was considerable support for Taiwan, and with a segment of U.S. voters that favors Taiwan. This could have created an impasse for Trump in seeking more amicable relations with China and might even impede a trade deal that Trump wants.

Obama's action may also be questioned about what good could come from the decision. Greater strategic coordination between U.S. forces and Taiwan's military will be enhanced. But was that needed? U.S. policy has long been to restrict the development of Taiwan's offensive capabilities vis-à-vis China in order to prevent Taipei from starting a war. U.S. arms sales to Taiwan reflect this clearly. So does America's policy of strategic ambiguity. Will changing this, which more contacts with Taiwan suggests, contribute to America's national interest or peace in the area? No argument has been offered that it would.

Clearly President Obama has made Taiwan a more contentious issue in United States-China relations and may well handicap Donald Trump.

A second matter is new anti-propaganda legislation, specifically the Countering Disinformation and Propaganda Act, President Obama also signed in the closing days of his presidency. Observers say it may "set the stage" for a war of ideas with China and may plague the coming Trump administration with problems it does not want.

The bill is backed by a special budget of $800 million that will be used to train journalists and give grants to non-governmental organizations, think tanks and consulting companies that decipher disinformation. This will create momentum that may be hard to control.

Senator Chris Murphy, a Democrat from Connecticut that co-drafted the legislation, addressed the "China threat" during debate on the bill. Meanwhile Chinese scholars opined that the bill could be used as a club against China.

The timing of the bill, not just President Obama signing it, also suggests it is aimed at China. Almost at the same time it got the presidential signature China's Central China Television announced the rebranding of China Global Television Network to consolidate its worldwide reach. This followed an earlier report the Chinese government had allocated $6.5 billion to spread China's message abroad.

It likewise happened amid recent reports China is "buying into" Hollywood in grand fashion. China's richest man, Wang Jianlin, (through his company the Dalian Wanda Group) already owns America's second largest theater chain and a major film maker and is engaged in talks to purchase Dick Clark Productions valued at $1 billion. This generated some bad vibes in Los Angeles and beyond.

While it has lots of money to expand its media influence and has been spending freely to do that, China is still not very competitive with the mainstream Western media. Furthermore, any influence it will have is diluted by other countries, especially Middle East nations, seeking a bigger media presence in the United States. Thus anxiety about China influencing public opinion in America thus seems overhyped.

Putting all of this in perspective, President Obama pledged to cooperate with President-elect Trump to make the transition a smooth one. However, in some critical ways he has done just the opposite. Clearly he has made conducting foreign relations with the most important nations in the world to the United States more challenging for Donald Trump when he becomes president.

FOUR

Why China Likes Donald Trump

History Tells Us Something

In 2016 there were a spate of articles in the Chinese media and blogs on the internet in China about which candidate for the U.S. presidency China and its people find the most interesting, the best for China, etc. Much of the discussion focused on the questions: Does China like Donald Trump? Do Chinese like Trump?

There is a difference in these two questions. The former refers to the Chinese government; the later means the Chinese people.

The Chinese government, as a general principle, does not comment on foreign elections and, in particular, does not express which candidate it prefers to win. Doing so is considered interfering in the domestic politics of another country, which China condemned during the period of imperialism and colonialism, and still does.

Therefore, government officials in China have rarely expressed their opinion about Donald Trump, notwithstanding his often-expressed provocative statements, including his condemning China for its lopsided trade balance with the United States (selling a lot more than it buys), which translates into lost jobs in America, and a number of other matters. Trump has even spoken of China's "economic rape" of the United States and its "Great Wall of protectionism."

In contrast, the Chinese media and bloggers, especially the youth in China, had a lot to say about "Donald." They appreciate and often laud his different and interesting style. They like the fact he speaks openly and candidly on political and other issues, which they say Chinese officials don't and wish they did.

Two months ago Sina Weibo, China's largest microblogging site, via the hashtag #SuperTuesday, attracted 13.5 million clicks and 5,600 comments. Donald Trump was the focus of attention. Subsequently, in a survey conducted by huanqiu.com netizens, Chinese respondents were asked if they liked Trump. More than 4,200, or 59.7 percent, said yes. Since huanqui.com is connected to the newspaper *Global Times* that is state-owned and nationalistic, this was a surprise but was also telling.

Some respondents reported that they like Trump's focus on economic issues, realizing that China's commercial relations with the United States had to be fixed, and noted that he is not so concerned about human rights and political freedoms in China and does not talk about military issues much. Also Trump opposes the Trans-Pacific Partnership deal that Chinese view as part of America's pivot to Asia. Both are seen as pointedly anti-China and as reflecting U.S. envy of China's successes.

However, some of the compliments registered by China's young people were actually subtle criticism or constitute warnings about Trump. Recently some have said they like him because, if elected, he would probably mess up America, especially U.S. foreign policy, and this would be an advantage to China. China would become the predominant power in the world as the United States falls into second place—a result of Trump's missteps and the likelihood he would alienate some important countries, including America's allies.

What is almost totally absent, however, from the heady discussions of Donald Trump are his political party, how China has viewed America's two political parties (and does now), and how that might relate to the issue at hand, namely Donald Trump's popularity. This backdrop is significant.

In this connection, Westerners think (and they are right) Chinese are students of history, with long memories, and people who connect the present with the past. Chinese also learn from their elders, and they network. Naturally affected are the views Chinese hold of Donald Trump and his adversary Hillary Clinton.

To the point, Chinese leaders, beginning with Mao and including high officials now, not to mention historians and Chinese scholars, have stated they like the Republican Party more than the Democratic Party.

They have good reasons.

The two American presidents that treated China the most dreadfully were Woodrow Wilson and Franklin Roosevelt—both Democrats.

At Versailles at the end of World War I, President Wilson, who had earlier promised China the return of Shandong Province, a German leasehold, acquiesced to Japan's demand for the territory—even though China had been an ally during the conflict. The prize involved was land that was the home of Confucius—sacred to most Chinese. China's ambassador to France at the time compared it to the way Christians view Jerusalem.

China considered President Wilson's action a betrayal of the first order and refused to become a signatory to the Treaty of Versailles.

Woodrow Wilson made other concessions at China's expense. Plus Wilson was also known for his racism (which has only recently gotten attention in the United States). Chinese came to despise Wilson and "his" League of Nations. Their ill feelings and deep ire toward Wilson marked the birth of anti-Western Chinese nationalism.

President Franklin Roosevelt was a friend and an adamant supporter of Chiang Kai-shek and purveyed him arms and other assistance during World War II, which Mao and his party charged were used to kill them and huge numbers of Chinese citizens, as Chiang was more interested in maintaining power than he was fighting the Japanese.

Also, during the Chinese Civil War that followed from 1945 to 1949 FDR continued to supply Chiang with weapons and other assistance, prolonging a war Chiang inevitably lost while killing countless more Chinese.

But worst of all FDR sold out, betrayed, China at Yalta at the end of World War II—granting the Soviet Union Chinese territory plus the use of Chinese ports. To most Chinese, this was pure chicanery; to some it was a new form of imperialism.

The two acts of perfidy, by Wilson and Roosevelt, in Chinese eyes, also resulted in the preservation of the Western system of international politics that contributed to further protracted conflicts and wars.

Democrats Truman, Kennedy and Johnson launched wars in Asia that cost China lives and treasure. They treated China as a pariah and an enemy. Chinese leaders do not see them in a positive light.

In contrast, Chinese leaders applaud President Nixon, a Republican, for engineering the historic breakthrough in United States-China relations. He and Secretary of State Kissinger are still revered for their accomplishments. Often mentioned is their espousing realism, which Chinese leaders say with regularity they understand and support.

President Reagan vastly improved Sino-American relations. George H.W. Bush was one of China's closest friends. In contrast China characterized President Carter as "weak-kneed" in dealing with the Soviet Union.

Under President Barack Obama United States-China relations have not been worse since before Nixon. Currently, ties are strained over what China regards as Washington deliberately pursuing anti-China policies in the East China Sea, the South China Sea and regarding cyber-warfare.

Regarding the South China Sea dispute, a noted U.S. diplomat, Charles Freeman, stated: "Our arguments relate to freedom of navigation. Yet this freedom has never been threatened or challenged." And "its most self-interested champion is China."

Michael Hayden, the only person to serve as both head of the U.S. Central Intelligence Agency and the National Security Agency has asserted: "We are better at stealing other people's secrets than anyone else in the world." If China were the foremost culprit engaging in cyber warfare against the United States, wouldn't Washington respond by doing the same, or worse, to China?

Chinese leaders perceive jealousy has motivated President Obama to obstruct China's one belt, one road plan that will "connect the world" (the biggest such project in history that will cost $1 trillion and help the economies of a host of developing nations). Obama has also tried to convince a number of nations not to join China's Asian Infrastructure Investment Bank, has sought to block the Chinese Yuan from becoming a global currency, and has given advice to the government of Thailand to turn down a Chinese proposal to build a canal across its southern peninsula.

Similarly Chinese leaders resent Hillary Clinton's once carrying the torch in criticizing China on human rights (though she has abandoned that in recent years). They also criticize the U.S. pivot to Asia, which was her creation that China views as an effort (though a futile one) to contain China, and they chide her support of Japan in its conflict with China over islands in the East China Sea.

Chinese leaders don't trust her.

Government officials in Beijing are skeptical of Donald Trump. He is an unknown. But they feel they can negotiate with him and need to resolve some economic disputes that have festered too long. They like him and his party better than Hillary and her party.

FIVE

President Trump's Decision to Honor the One-China Policy

How Best to Explain It?

The evening of February 9, in a telephone conversation with China's President Xi Jinping, U.S. President Donald Trump made a volte-face from his previous statements and pledged to honor America's one-China policy. According to the White House, Trump's decision was made at President Xi's request.

President Trump's change of heart (or policy) appeared to erase the hostile disposition of United States-China relations that followed his telephone call from Taiwan's President Tsai Ing-wen in early December and his subsequent statements to the effect America's one-China policy was not necessarily his policy and furthermore was negotiable.

It may be that Trump's tête-à-tête with Xi was more important than simply the two leaders resolving the one-China issue—though that was certainly important. It included the two leaders inviting the other to visit their country. It seemed to represent détente following more than a month of hostile exchanges. It could be lasting.

How does one account for Trump's turnaround?

The U.S. media and various pundits explained that Donald Trump's hostility toward China prior to his becoming president was simply campaign rhetoric to be discarded once he was in office. This follows the example of previous presidents.

Alternatively President Trump's new persona reflected the fact that after some pondering about it he grasped the reality that China is vitally important to him and to the United States. China is the world's second largest economy and its largest trading nation, the holder of more than a trillion dollars in U.S. debt, the planet's major provider of economic help to developing countries and the dominant global builder (which Trump could certainly appreciate).

Another explanation is that Trump had sought to convey the message that he would not be bullied by China as Barack Obama and some other U.S. presidents had been. And he accomplished that. Or, some of his critics depicted Trump as a novice in managing foreign affairs; he needed to correct that impression as well, and to some extent he did.

President Xi's situation also provides explanations.

Xi grasped the reasons behind Trump's earlier questioning one-China and his now accepting it. China had taken advantage of Barack Obama when he became president and that did not end well. In addition, the Western media hated Trump and sought to ambush him on foreign policy issues; Trump needed to show some mettle. The Western media also disliked cum hated Xi and China so President Xi knew what that was about.

China's president also faced some vexing domestic problems: a slowing economy, local government and corporate debt (which the International Monetary Fund warned risked sparking a serious crisis), money flight from China, the stalling of reforms (including Xi's anti-corruption drive that witnessed pushback from local governments) and more. Plus, he was preparing for a landmark Chinese Communist Party congress in a few months. A continuing feud with Trump in this context was an unwanted distraction.

President Xi certainly wanted to avoid trade problems with the United States. A trade war would hurt everyone; though it would probably hurt China more than the United States. He appreciated Trump's complaints about the unsustainable U.S. trade deficit with China and Trump's demand China do something to reign in North Korea.

But these explanations may be too simplistic. . . .

Certainly there is more to say about Trump-Xi relations, their understandings (and sympathies) of each other, and their, in many ways, similar worldviews.

The day that Donald Trump took the famous (or infamous) telephone call from Taiwan's President Tsai Ing-wen that set in motion his questioning the one-China policy and several weeks of strained Sino-American relations, Trump met with Henry Kissinger. Kissinger then departed on a trip to China. After he returned the two met again.

One rendering of the Trump-Kissinger get together followed by Kissinger's meeting with President Xi was that Kissinger was a go-between or mediator. He advised Xi on Trump's situation, the reasons for his speaking to President Tsai and his motives for challenging the one-China policy. He suggested Xi not take Trump's talk too seriously and "bark back" if he wished (Trump expected it) and relations would be fine after a short period of tension.

To Kissinger there was logic behind Trump's otherwise apparently reckless talk and actions.

Kissinger had written about the pending failure, cum collapse, of the international order in his book *World Order.* He propounded on the importance of working United States-China relations to prevent a system breakdown. Xi had written something similar in his book *The Governance of China.* Trump had called the global system unsustainable. All three seemed to be on the same page.

Richard Haass, president of the Council on Foreign Relations, said to be the conscience of U.S. government officials in charge of foreign policy, offered a strong supporting opinion. In a just published book, *A World in Disarray,* Haass wrote of "one historical era ending and another beginning."

Indeed the post-World War II world order or the Western "liberal democratic global system" whose ingredients were free trade, almost universal economic and social development, progress in human rights, a major functional role for the United Nations and other international institutions, respect for international law, and nuclear non-proliferation, was now dying.

President Trump's believed the inevitable shift to a new world order could not be evolutionary; it had to be profound, even revolutionary. Moreover, it could best grow out of turmoil or crisis. One analyst described Trump's method as "calculated chaos."

President Xi could certainly understand this. It was the way his party had come to power in China. Chinese were taught precisely this when they studied China's history. It was Deng Xiaoping's method to reform China's economic and political systems after Mao died.

Could Trump and Xi cooperate to create a new global order? It seemed they could.

President Xi had recently moved to correct the trade imbalance with the United States—preliminarily at least. He took some strong action against North Korea, as Trump said he should. President Trump dumped former president Obama's policy of trying to isolate, cum contain, China by appealing to other countries not to support China's number one global building project, the new Silk Road and its attendant maritime "road," and China's financial organizations designed to promote global economic development. Trump sought to build with China, not against China.

Trump and Xi were likeminded in terms of the paramount actors in the coming new international order. They are China and the United States. Europe, Japan and Russia were declining powers and would play but marginal roles—though Russia due to its strategic power (nuclear weapons) was in that way an exception.

The world is thus headed toward a fresh (or revised) bipolarity. Even though China, and many others, applauded the coming of a multipolar world that was not in the cards. Nor was it desirable. As Haass notes it is too complicated. Certainly, if power balancing is to be a critical element of a multipolar system, it would not appear to be able to function well given a host asymmetries including the fact that in military power terms Europe had little to no influence on China.

Clearly Trump's election victory and his perspective of creating chaos to clear the path to important (and historic) decisions comport with the view the current world order is about to end. Some historians, in fact, view Trump's election victory as introducing a "permanent shift" and even the creation of a "new America" as happened in 1828 under President Andrew Jackson, in 1860 with Lincoln, in 1896 and William McKinley, and in 1932 because of FDR. Times changed as conditions required but leaders made it happen.

There is a parallel case to be made for China. Xi Jinping is a seminal president. He has given himself new powers and has orchestrated a new strongman leader style of rule to supplant collective leadership. This comes at a critical time when China was at a fork in the road and must decide whether to fully challenge the current world order and make a genuine bid for global leadership. In fact, Xi has made this move. Recently he vowed to lead the "new world order."

More specifically President Xi sought to realize the "China dream" he had talked a lot about. He wants to restore China's past splendor.

What are Donald Trump's dreams? Who are his models? Andrew Jackson? Both railed against the elite establishment. Both changed the course of U.S. history. The establishment reviled both. Jackson was a "leader for the common man" president; so is Trump. But President Jackson reigned a long time ago and there is much dissimilarity between then and now.

Some say President Nixon, who made a difference with a unique foreign policy strategy. But current conditions are not like 1969. President Reagan? Reagan orchestrated the end of the Cold War. But challenging the liberal world order now is different.

Harvard University Historian Niall Ferguson suggests Trump's mentor is Theodore Roosevelt. President Roosevelt fought against corruption in Washington, DC. He was an individualist with a plan, a nationalist that sought to promote America's greatness, an advocate of balance of power and a power broker. He was a builder (Panama Canal). He saw the U.K. as a close ally and friend.

Teddy Roosevelt had no regard for the liberal world order that praised peace treaties and international organizations that built collective security on expensive American obligations. International order, to TR, was to be based on strong leaders and regional blocs lead by great men.

Coincidently, or not, President Xi is viewed by some to be a modern Teddy Roosevelt. He is battling corruption in government as Roosevelt did. He is a navy man. He admires Admiral Mahan. He seeks to make China a regional power through maritime clout while conceding influence to the United States (as Roosevelt did to the British navy) at least for a while.

A United States-China "relationship" (the world being a Sino-American condominium, a reconstructed bipolar system) has much to say for itself. It has been talked about already. The terms Chinamerica and G-2 reflect that.

This would marginalize Europe and Japan, which seems inevitable anyway. Such a system would focus attention on critical world order issues. It would be effective in dealing with terrorism, which is the scourge of both countries and the world. It would unlikely oversee a new world war. Washington-Beijing cooperation based on the mutual recognition of China's financial superiority and America's military dominance represents realism. Collaboration would also help make this arrangement work.

Perhaps the problems of a crumbling world order can be resolved in this way. That would be a good thing. President Trump's accepting the one-China perspective is a beginning.

SIX

The Challenge of China's Role as the World's Builder

For some years, the two biggest challenges China's external aid and investments have presented to the United States came from the huge amount of money China possessed and employed to provide financial help to developing countries and the fact China did not comply with the Western definitions (and rules) of aid and investing.

Now there is a new challenge. As a result of it applying its monetary resources via aid and investments and the expertise it has acquired by building at home to constructing roads, railroads, dams, communications facilities, pipelines, ports, economic zones and more to projects abroad, China has won the title of the "world's builder."

America was once the world's "connector": building the Panama Canal and other super-sized projects while bringing the world together by constructing railroads, road, etc. and via aid and trade. That is no more.

In two special ways China has increased its influence that is vexing to the United States.

One, it has built pipelines into Russia and Central Asia as well as through Burma to South China and is looking at one to pass through Pakistan. This diminishes the importance of the U.S Navy in protecting China's oil lifeline to the Middle East, which made China beholden to the United States and willing to make concessions to Washington on other issues.

Second, China has come to control the world economy to a significant degree. In the first decade of this century, China became the world's leading nation in attracting foreign investments and in exporting goods and services, while its imprint on contributing to the planetary product became the largest of any country. In 2013 China became the world's biggest trading nation.

This means that the United States is no longer the axis of the world's economic activity. It had held that honor since World War II.

The impact of this is now underscored, and amplified, by China's Herculean efforts to rebuild and expand (actually transform it into a modern transportation system) its ancient Silk Road and add to it a maritime route, the combined effort being known as the one belt, one road (OBOR) project. Launched originally as an action plan, it is now being put into operation and has already gained the status of the world's largest ever such project.

The one belt, one road project was to span more than 60 countries representing 40% of the world's gross domestic product. It will involve and link up countries in Northeast Asia, Southeast Asia, South Asia, Central Asia, the Middle East, Europe and Africa. It will create a situation of "All roads lead to Beijing." It will generate mutual dependency between China and other countries—more on the part of other countries because China is economically so much larger and is the world's foremost trading country. It will give China considerable control over the world's transport, both on land and on sea.

China, it was estimated, would expend $1 trillion on the effort. Together with China's Asian Infrastructure Investment Bank's contribution, which will put billions of dollars into road building and other related projects, the total of China's financial contribution to "bring the world together" was reported to be $1.25 trillion or more in just nine years. Putting this into perspective America's vaunted Marshall Plan to facilitate the economic recovery of Europe after the war, in today's dollars, was just over $100 billion.

Some nations and regions deserve special mention in assessing the impact of China's building efforts.

Pakistan is the sixth largest country in the world by population. It is the second largest Islamic country. It is one of the world's seven nuclear powers. It is critical geopolitically to the United States in its war on terrorism, being adjacent to Afghanistan, and for its influence among Islamic nations. It has been the top recipient of China's aid and investments in recent years.

Building projects related to OBOR in Pakistan has dramatically increased China's influence there. At present China is in the process of distributing $46 billion more in funds to construct roads, railroads, pipelines, hydro and other energy projects, most of which are a part of the vaunted "economic corridor" that ties Pakistan from the Indian Ocean to China's southwest. This eclipses U.S. financial assistance to Pakistan.

There are also side effects. Two years ago China's trade with Pakistan was $16 billion, up 12 percent from the previous year. Both were around triple the figures for United States-Pakistan trade. Pakistan has been much more friendly toward China as a result, while U.S. influence has waned.

China's aid and investments in building have profoundly impacted every country in Southeast Asia. China is a major trading partner of all countries in the region. China's work on the Mekong River project and fast train lines linking all of the countries of Mainland Southeast Asia to China have helped Beijing expand its influence in the region.

The result is the only marginal success the United States has had in getting support for its policy of trammeling China's involvement in the South China Sea and its efforts to build closer relations with Vietnam, Burma, and the Philippines. The three cannot ignore China's Leviathan economy, its role as a trading partner, and its importance as a builder. Plus China is close-by.

American strategists have long felt they could disrupt China's relations with the Soviet Union as the United States did in the late 1960s and after. But China's money and its building railroads and pipelines have helped Russia financially and have kept the two close allies to the chagrin of Washington. The "alliance" also makes it harder for the United States to challenge China in the North China Sea and the South China Sea.

China's building, together with its aid and investments, in Mongolia and the countries of Central Asia—like its roads, railroads and pipelines in Pakistan and Burma—have helped China acquire needed energy and natural resources without using sea transport. China has also found new markets for its products.

Africa is included in the Maritime Silk Road. China is also separately developing roads, railroads, dams, communications facilities, pipelines, ports, and economic zones on the continent. Almost every African country is a beneficiary of China's building. In fact, China's financial help has given Africa an unprecedented growth rate, making it the second fastest-growing region in the world (after Asia). African leaders regularly praise and thank China for this.

Latin America is not left out. China is building roads, railroads, pipelines, etc. in America's backyard. A region that used to be America's exclusive sphere of influence is no more.

China is also into future giant projects (besides the one road, one belt one), once the purview of other nations—especially the United States. It has proposed new canals to link the Atlantic and Pacific oceans. China has discussed with the government of Thailand building a canal across the 30-mile Kra Isthmus in the southern part of the country. The Kra Canal would become a link in China's maritime silk road and shave the transport costs from the Middle East and South Asia to the Far East.

Beijing's leaders have even broached the idea of building an undersea tunnel to Taiwan and one under the Bering Sea to connect Asia and North America. Its Bohai Strait tunnel launched in April this year to connect two areas in North China by ultra-fast trains will provide the experience.

China is also a world leader in advancing green energy. It builds dams, nuclear power plants and solar farms. It is embarrassing that it has assumed a central role in these realms when the United States preaches clean renewable energy.

China has funneled much of its aid and investments through three regional organizations that China controls or influences: the Shanghai Cooperation Organization, the Association of Southeast Asian Nations, and the Forum on China-Africa Cooperation. All of these organizations are large in terms of the nations participating and their total economic impact. America holds membership in none of them. (Incidentally, regional economic bodies in recent years have largely overshadowed the efforts of global organizations in promoting economic growth.)

The success China has had in building and the global reputation it has attained for it have greatly enhanced China's global power and influence—mainly at the expense of the United States. As a result, the Obama administration has reacted negatively.

President Obama tried to persuade other nations not to join China's Asian Infrastructure Investment Bank. But he did not succeed. Most Asian countries have gladly participated. Even U.S. allies, such as the U.K., have ignored Obama's plea.

Ditto with President Obama's call to not permit the Chinese currency, the Yuan, to become a global currency (as this would amplify China's financial influence throughout the world and diminish the role of the U.S dollar). Meanwhile the Yuan became one of the "core currencies" making up the International Monetary Fund's Special Drawing Rights or SDRs, often called the "IMF's currency" or the "global money."

President Obama's moves seem to reflect pique or a reaction based on jealousy and the United States being upstaged by China. It may also relate to Obama's concern over his legacy.

Many observers note Obama's (originating from Secretary of State Clinton in 2011) Asian pivot, is the only tenet of his foreign policy that might deserve being tagged a doctrine, and it has failed. Some considered it a reactionary anti-China containment policy. Many labeled it a strategic (military) policy that is a zero-sum (my gain is your loss) construct. Asians preferred a non-zero-sum system based on economic relations.

President Obama has added an economic "leg"—the Trans-Pacific Partnership agreement. It was designed to limit China's influence over world trade. But it was slow to develop and by 2016, with both of the U.S. presidential candidates opposing it, it was a dead issue.

One might wish the United States, with its long-time commitment to assist developing countries to enjoy economic growth, to cooperate with China rather than obstruct.

SEVEN

The First Trump-Xi Meeting

Success or Failure?

In April 2017 U.S. President Donald Trump and China's President Xi Jinping met for the first time in Mar-a-Lago, Florida (Trump's "Southern Whitehouse) for a two day conference. The meeting was portrayed as an important, perhaps even a milestone, meeting.

However, even before the meeting ended some U.S. media talking heads labeled the meeting a failure. They had two reasons for saying this.

One, there was no communiqué, much less a treaty, to come out of the conference. There was not even an announcement of its major accomplishments. Since there no releases of deals reached the U.S. liberal media said the meeting was a bust.

Two, during dinner on the second day of the conference President Trump informed President Xi that he had just ordered a missile strike on an air force base in Syria in response to the Syrian regime using sarin gas to kill its opponents (including children and even babies). President Xi was, to say the least, surprised. Some said he was upset.

To grasp whether this is a true picture one must first note that the U.S. media are highly partisan (more than anytime in recent history) and are comprised of an inordinately high percent of Trump haters. The U.S. media also is biased against China, figuring a rising China (which China certainly is) will dominate the future world order and that will spell an end to the West's global system the media likes.

Thus the media reported in a negative fashion on the event.

Another criterion, arguably a better one, to gauge whether the meeting succeeded or not, is to ask: what were the hopes and goals of the participants going into the confab? What did Trump and Xi want? Were they pleased with the outcomes of the event?

President Xi's objectives were to have a good first get-together with President Trump, the world's most important leader, and dampen speculation that they would not get along or that there were explosive issues that divided them and the two countries.

This was crucial to President Xi because he would convene a landmark meeting of the Chinese Communist Party in the fall. At this party congress there would be vital personnel changes and certain new policies would be enshrined, including continuing the anti-corruption drive Xi had launched after the last congress in 2012, economic growth targets (that linked to unemployment, trade and more), decisions on China's major foreign policy goals, and much more.

President Xi calculated that a convivial meeting with President Trump would make his party congress go easier and end better. It would improve his image as a world leader.

President Xi did not bring any big specific issues in Sino-American relations that he aimed to resolve during his meeting with President Trump.

President Trump did have specific objects in his vest pocket when he met with President Xi: fixing their trade imbalance (that connected to creating jobs and fixing the U.S. huge debt), easing tensions in the South China Sea (that required China's help), and getting Beijing to assist Washington in dealing with North Korea's bad behavior in doing nuclear weapons' and missile tests.

But President Trump did not expect a deal in the form of a communiqué, written accord, or even a Chinese public announcement. What he wanted was for China to take some action on these three matters in the near future. Trump had reason for optimism that he would get something, perhaps quite a lot, from China.

The notion that President Trump shocked President Xi in announcing the missile attacks on Syria, and may have even embarrassed Xi, cannot be denied. But was it really serious?

President Xi is known to be a leader that can handle surprises. Clearly he is a person with aplomb and the ability to stay in control. Plus Henry Kissinger reportedly told him during a visit to China late last year that Donald Trump is brusque and often says and does unexpected things but that he is someone Xi can deal with. So he was probably prepared for the surprise.

Then, one must ask this question: Would it have been better for President Trump not to have told his counterpart then or immediately thereafter? In Xi's mind hiding or even Trump delaying saying what he had done would probably not have been a mark of friendship or an expression of confidence in their relationship.

Anyway, China does not approve of the use of poison gas to kill people. In fact, it acceded to the 1925 Geneva Convention outlawing its use more than six decades ago. Also China cares about promoting a positive global image. Lastly China has no serious involvement in the civil conflict in Syria and President Xi was not, judging from the way the meeting proceeded, put off by Trump's action.

Another relevant fact is that neither President Trump nor President Xi wanted to create unrealistic expectations about United States-China relations. The two nations are competitors, big time competitors. Some observers even believe the so-called Thucydides Trap (the inevitability of the status quo power and its challenger going to war) applies to current Sino-United States relations.

Yet both leaders are fully aware of the reality that the other is vitally important and their relationship will determine whether the global financial system works, proliferation and terrorism are controlled, and much more. Their working together is a *sine qua non* for international interactions to operate efficiently.

In addition, one must keep in mind that President Xi preferred Donald Trump to Hillary Clinton (and no doubt still does), that President Trump has not made an issue of China's human rights or governance (that previous presidents did and which China did not appreciate), that Trump has spoken highly of China's efforts to "build the world" (in fact has approved of the United States joining that effort, which President Obama opposed) and that under Obama United States-China relations had not been as bad since before the Nixon administration.

Another factor is President Trump has expressed great admiration for China including its recent accomplishments (which to many in the West evoke apprehension). Chinese leaders deeply appreciated this.

Before the close of the event, Trump's granddaughter, whom he has encouraged to learn Chinese (in fact, she speaks it daily) sang in Chinese and recited Tang Dynasty poetry before President Xi and First Lady Peng Liyuan. This, onlookers said, was the highlight of their trip. One witness remarked that from this Chinese realized Trump deeply respected China and its culture and wanted to be China's friend.

After the meeting President Trump spoke of the tremendous goodwill and friendship it generated and the "great honor" to have President Xi and the First Lady visit. President Xi and the Chinese media expressed delight over the meeting and optimism about United States-China relations.

Though the meeting was mainly a get-to-know-each-other encounter, the two leaders did talk issues of substance and even made some decisions on work to be done: on cyber security, law enforcement, a code of safe conduct affecting naval and military encounters. The two leaders agreed on a 100-day plan to address the trade issue, as President Trump wanted.

President Trump wanted to make deals (arguable the best way to carry on foreign relations with China) and believed he could. He thus graciously accepted President Xi's invitation to visit China in the fall.

Finally, there was a critical (but largely unnoticed) "meeting of the minds" between the two presidents at the meeting. One might even say there was an "ideological convergence"; pragmatism permeated the meeting.

All of this suggests a good beginning, which is what the meeting was supposed to be. Results to follow…

EIGHT

Has President Trump's Worldview Become More Discernible?

During the presidential election campaign the U.S. media parsed, assessed and attempted to categorize Donald Trump's foreign policy statements. Likewise his pronouncements and actions after he became president. They have endeavored to reach some conclusions about a Trump strategy or even a "Trump Doctrine." They have not been very successful.

There are several ways to explain this.

First, President Trump does not want to signal what he will do or what decisions he is likely to make in the realm of foreign affairs. He said so. He wants to be unpredictable, inscrutable. That is his *modus operandi*. He also perceives that President Obama made a big mistake in announcing what his next moves were to enemies abroad, who could then prepare countermoves.

Second, President Trump feels it is all right to change his mind in foreign policy making. He should keep his promises at home. Americans elected him go do that, and he has. External affairs are a different matter.

Third, he seeks to use bluff and intimidation to realize his foreign policy goals. This works better if the opponent is off guard.

Fourth, to President Trump foreign policy should be conducted through negotiations. That means talking and reaching deals, refusing or declining deals as a tactic, and using pressure and threats with military power as a backup to get things done.

Having said this and judging from President Trump's foreign policy activities, how he interacts with foreign leaders, deals he has attained, his launching a missile attack on a base in Syria, his meeting with China's President Xi at Mar-a-Lago all give further evidence about how Donald

Trump thinks about conducting foreign affairs and perhaps even how he views the world.

Judging from his focus on making deals and building up U.S. military forces to facilitate negotiations, President Trump espouses a realist view of the world. That means power and influence are the essence of effective foreign policy making.

He is not an idealist. He puts little stock in promoting lofty principles. He doesn't talk of human rights. He is not intent on promoting democracy. He even denies wanting to orchestrate regime change or getting involved in other countries' domestic affairs as was the error of the Bush administration.

He doesn't mind talking to leaders of other countries no matter their or their country's moral turpitude. He has met with Russian leaders. He even said he would meet with North Korea's Kim Jong-un. His goal is to advance the U.S. national interest, not proselytize. This is further evidence of Trump's realist thinking.

During the campaign President Trump was labeled an isolationist, a non-interventionist and a nationalist president. He was also seen as a Russophile that sought to use close relations with Moscow to help expand U.S. global influence.

His missile attack on Syria changed this narrative. He is no longer seen as a non-interventionist. His military budget, the largest increase in military expenditures of any president for some years, has labeled him an internationalist. In particular Trump wants more ships for the navy—which is the main instrument for showing the U.S. flag abroad. This seems to come straight from Admiral Alfred Mahan, who linked naval power and global authority in his famous book *The Influence of Sea Power upon History*.

In the wake of the missile attack President Trump spoke favorably of alliances. (During the campaign he questioned the value of NATO and some other defense agreements.) But since then he has promoted ties with allies.

Allies will help President Trump employ pressure to realize foreign policy goals. Also they would strengthen his hand if he needs to use military force.

Trump citing a moral argument when justifying his missile attack on Syria (the Assad regime killing civilians, even babies, with poison gas) indicates the president will make legal and ethical behavior an issue if and when he needs to. This can sometimes complement realist policies.

President Trump's meeting with China's President Xi Jinping at this time indicates he seeks good relations with *the* world's rising power and its predominant economic player. Trump accomplished productive negotiations with Xi. The two countries now appear to be working together and may even be seen as friends.

One may discern something about President Trump's worldview from all of this.

His realism and his new relationship with President Xi suggest he sees the world as bipolar. The two global powers are the United States and China. The United States is the military power. (Trump's increasing the military budget, now even faster than China, ensures this will last—not to mention the fact the United States has numerous allies while China has few.) China, the world's number one trading nation, with immense financial clout and a reputation for building all over the world, is the global economic leader.

This may suggest an asymmetric relationship. But China needs the United States to protect it far-flung trade, aid and building. Anyway Chinese leaders deny China is ready to be a world military power. The United States needs China's financial cooperation and even perhaps its help. President Trump has declared he wants to work with China to build and maintain a stable global financial system. (President Obama opposed doing this.)

There has been talk of the international system evolving into a multipolar structure. But the other powers are all in decline. Russia suffers from a shrinking population and its economy is in the doldrums. Japan and Europe have the same problems. India, which is doing well economically, is still way behind the United States and China in economic size and is basically a regional power militarily speaking.

Might Trump seek to return the global system to a unipolar one? No! He has shown no inclination to favor the Neocon's view of the world. Anyway, the time for that has passed.

A universal system? Trump views the United Nations as effete, corrupt, wasteful, useless and even hopeless. He found the UN unable to help him deal with the Syria crisis, so he acted alone. He does not want to put more money into the UN or rely on it for much.

What about what international relations scholar Morton Kaplan once called a "unit-veto system"? Kaplan suggested countries with nuclear weapons had special prerogatives. Trump's statements of wanting to go further with keeping Iran from nuclear weapons than the Obama deal and his calls to denuclearize North Korea, suggest that he does not accept such a system (or such a characteristic of the global order) and instead wants non-proliferation—which top world leaders have advocated for some time.

What about the Thucydides Trap? This lesson comes from historians, reinforced by scholars pushing game theory and others. It says the major power (and status quo regime), meaning the United States, will be challenged by the rising power (especially if a fast rising power), which is China, and war will result. This means that a bipolar (the United States and China) system will be unstable and ultimately dangerous.

But there are two reasons to believe a United States-China war will not happen.

First, this proposition applies to the past better than to recent history. The bipolar system of the Cold War period did not result in war. Mutual Assured Destruction seemed to have precluded that. Plus cooperation or collusion.

Second, the United States and China and their leaders (in particular President Trump and President Xi) respect each other much more than the U.S and Soviet Union and their leaders did during the Cold War. Also they have some important things in common: Neither is enamored with the liberal world order that is based on military power. Both have read Sun Tzu's *The Art of War* that teaches that the greatest victory is won without fighting.

To return to the original question about Trump's foreign policy strategy or a doctrine, President Trump does not want to tell us what he is thinking. But in some ways he has.

President Trump's worldview as it is evolving seems to hinge on good United States-China relations, as it should given these are the two major global powers present and future.

Trump wants to keep the peace through good communications and pursuing mutual benefits.

NINE

Does the United States Expect Too Much of China in Dealing with North Korea?

The "North Korea problem"—meaning North Korea's threats to use its missiles and nuclear weapons against South Korea, Japan and/or the United States and set off a global conflagration—demands a solution. The narrative heard in the United States and pretty much around the world is that China holds the key.

North Korea, it is argued, is very dependent on China economically and in other ways. In fact, it is commonly said and reported in the Western media Beijing has such leverage over Pyongyang that it can persuade cum force North Korea to desist from testing its nuclear weapons and missiles and even get rid of them.

But China has done little. Arguably it can and should do much more.

This account is partly true, partly exaggerated, and partly false. Furthermore, China's policies and its national interests are misunderstood and/or are ignored and Beijing has been given little credit for what it has done and is doing.

What is true about the narrative?

The pitch that North Korea is heavily reliant on China's financial aid (including investments that are not expected to be repaid) and trade is true. One might even say that North Korea is linked at the hip to China economically and cannot do without China.

China has, varying from year to year, provided upward of 70 percent of North Korea's energy and consumer goods and a large portion of its food aid. China is by far North Korea's biggest trading partner—at times equal to or ahead of all of its other contacts combined.

North Korea's dependency on China for sure buys Beijing influence with the North Korean government. China has been allowed an in-country presence to construct aid and investment projects. China has even been granted the right to station its troops in North Korea to protect its investments and ensure refugees do not cross the border into China.

Indeed China can influence North Korea's policies and its behavior.

What is exaggerated about the narrative of North Korea's ties to China? Also, what is misunderstood?

North Korea has never become as submissive to China's wishes as one might suppose. North Korean leaders have not taken China's advice to reform its economy toward a free market and open trade regime and/or capitalist incentives. It has not stopped North Korea from engaging in terrorism (which China clearly does not approve of). It has not heeded China's warnings about its nuclear weapons and missile tests.

In fact, North Korean officials have frequently expressed unfriendliness toward China. Reportedly Kim Jong-un did not consult China before doing its recent nuclear weapons and missile tests. On occasion North Korean leaders have even they can get along easier with President Trump than Chinese officials. And there have been reports of the North Korean government overseeing or at least turning a blind eye to kidnapping Chinese citizens for ransom.

For their part Chinese leaders regard North Korea as obdurate and ungrateful and its leaders unhinged. They say openly that North Korea is a menace to world peace. Many Chinese officials are convinced they can do little to change this. Alas, Chinese pressure on North Korea to change on many matters has been, and is, ineffective.

This has been more pronounced in recent months. Recently Chinese citizens visiting North Korea report local police threaten them if they offer food to North Koreans suffering from malnutrition.

How are China's policies toward North Korea misunderstood?

China has important national interests at stake in its relationship with North Korea. These interests are not well understood by the United States and the global community. Nor are the likely results of China's actions to get North Korea to change dramatically.

In any case China applying strict sanctions against North Korea would cause widespread deprivation, even starvation, in North Korea. Though it would be difficult to predict the final results. Worse North Korean behavior? More terrorism? More extortion? The collapse of the government? An army coup?

Prolonged sanctions would very likely result in China experiencing a refugee dilemma—possibly millions of North Koreans fleeing across the border into China. The way to deal with it might be to mine the border and/or shoot people who cross it and violate China's sovereignty. The expected reaction from the liberal Western media and probably many

Western leaders would be a resounding condemnation of China for its actions.

China's most salient concern is a North Korean regime's collapse. North Korea currently serves as a buffer zone between China and U.S. forces in South Korea that might move north to a position just across the Yalu River if the North Korean regime imploded. (One need recall the last time this happened—in 1950—and the results.)

There are nearly 30 thousand U.S. military personnel in South Korea. A unified Korea governed by South Korea is definitely not something Chinese leaders would welcome (or tolerate) for strategic reasons. China would likely act to prevent it.

U.S. Secretary of State Tillerson pledged that it is not the intention of the United States to see regime change in North Korea or Korea's unification. America only wants a denuclearized, peaceful North Korea, he proclaimed.

But can Chinese leaders believe this? They have heard this before. They have also observed the United States, over a period of two-plus decades, make concessions (that many observers called appeasement), promises and threats to get North Korea to moderate its behavior. None produced positive results; in fact, the situation got worse.

Will President Trump's policy be different? Chinese leaders have good reason to think it will be. But they are also hesitant. After all the Democratic Party, half of Republicans, the media, Hollywood and academe in America oppose nearly everything Trump does and almost daily there are calls to investigate and/or impeach him.

America also demands North Korea stop selling nuclear weapons and missiles including technology of any kind to other countries. But North Korea sorely needs the money it makes from this, estimated to amount to US$1.5 billion annually (9 percent of North Korea's gross domestic product).

Washington has said little about how North Korea is to manage economically if the sanctions are continued or strengthened. Is China to provide it increased financial help? When? Not now, but later? Under what conditions?

The United States also wants North Korea to open up and join the rest of the world. But North Korea is a very closed country and its citizens know very little about the world. The government would likely be imperiled and might even fall if its citizens were to learn what its rulers have told them throughout their lifetimes is not true and the degree they have been kept from the pleasures and excitement of the modern world.

What is left out of the narrative and what is untrue about China's help to North Korea and its consequent influence?

China's foreign aid to North Korea in the past was provided at great cost and sacrifice to China. Why? North Korea was important to China given the perceived threat level to China in Northeast Asia. North Korea was China's only formal ally (with which it had, and still has, a security treaty).

China's aid to North Korea also helped to prevent at least to some degree Pyongyang from engaging in terrorism and practicing extortion that were an important means to sustain its economy. North Korean leaders even said this.

At times Beijing took direct punitive actions toward North Korea to pressure it to stop its reckless behavior. When Macao (a former Portuguese colony) became part of China in 1999 North Korean laundering counterfeit U.S. hundred dollar bills there ceased. On one occasion China cut off oil supplies to North Korea to express its dissatisfaction with its provocative policies.

In recent months, in the wake of North Korea conducting more nuclear tests, including a hydrogen bomb test (that constitutes a major escalation of its capacity to do harm to other countries), and its missile tests (proving it can hit countries further away and with greater accuracy), and what appeared to be new resolve on the part of the United States and the United Nations to finally do something, China moved the needle in its policy to help stem North Korea's provocations.

China signed on to UN resolutions applying severe sanctions against North Korea. This was a critical decision for Beijing and it gave the sanctions teeth they would not have had otherwise. China also adopted other trade actions to punish Pyongyang. According to some estimates this will impact ninety percent of North Korea's exports.

China did this in spite of appeals by North Korea that it not so act. What was North Korea thinking? One, if Kim Jong-Un gave up his nuclear weapons and missiles he would meet a fate similar to Muammar al-Qaddafi when he surrendered his nuclear program—being bombed by the United States and its allies and then being executed by his opponents. Two, North Korea "only wants to be treated fairly," like India and Pakistan that are no longer the targets of global pressure to scrap their weapons of mass destruction arsenals.

Also China has made domestic sacrifices to do what it did. The areas in China adjacent to North Korea have lost revenues from exports; this has hurt their economies, which were already in poor shape (part of China's rust belt). Beijing even forfeited diplomatic support from some Third World countries.

China has taken other measures to help the U.S. deal with North Korea. During the course of rising tensions between the United States and North Korea Chinese leaders met with the U.S. chairman of the Joint Chiefs of Staff, General Joseph Dunford Jr. and established a new military communications mechanism. This dampens the argument made by President Trump's opponents that his policies are liable to lead to war with China.

Chinese leaders evidently see that they can no longer gain any advantage by exploiting North Korea's antics that have destabilized Northeast Asia in some important ways to China's disadvantage, including driving South Korea and Japan to enhance their military power (and even think about going nuclear).

Another reason for Chinese leaders to support President Trump is that the Western media does not like China and is hypercritical of its government on human rights matters, pollution, control over the Internet, etc. while saying less or even ignoring these problems in other countries. President Trump is different.

In conclusion, China has changed its policies toward North Korea to comport with U.S. objectives. But China has received little acclaim. If the North Korea crisis is defused without military confrontation China must be given much credit.

TEN

Opponents and Supporters of China's One Belt One Road Project

In May 2017 year, China's President Xi Jinping convened the One Belt One Road (OBOR) Forum to mark the grand opening of what some observers labeled the "Project of the Century." It was truly an historic event.

Launched in 2013, OBOR was an essential element of President Xi's "China Dream." Xi sought, through the project, to transform China from an adapter to a driver of globalization and realize what some called China's plan for a worldwide "strategic economy." He intended to tie together 60 percent of the world's population and a third of its gross domestic product (GDP).

President Xi's plan has been effectively realized. More than 110 nations and international organizations attended the Forum. Most wanted to, and agreed to, become active participants.

The belt part of OBOR was to be the "rebuilt" Silk Road of yesteryear made up of super-fast trains, expressways and pipelines accompanied by new towns, factory complexes and more along the way. It will connect China and Europe and what is in between.

The road part will consist of new "super" sea-lanes between China and Europe connecting the Middle East, Africa, South Asia and Southeast Asia along the way. With its foreign aid and foreign investments China had already built seaports, adjunct airports, pipelines, highways, railroads and more along the maritime "road." Still more was to come.

Some called OBOR China's way to build a new Chinese empire. The model is America's extensive building effort after World War II. This helped the United States became financially the strongest nation on earth. China wants to do the same. A second objective is to make China's rise a peaceful one. In other words, China can climb to global preeminence without fighting any wars—the strategy China's famous strategist Sun Tzu advised in his book *The Art of War.*

But China's OBOR has its detractors and opponents. To some it is an existential threat. Given its Leviathan economic stature this is no wonder. Of course, OBOR also had its enthusiasts and supporters.

Detractors and/or opponents of OBOR included the Obama administration and now what is left of it or Obama supporters in the United States. Also Western media, Europe, India and Japan have expressed opposition.

Supporters are the Trump administration, Russia, a host of developing countries, and most countries along the two routes.

President Obama sought to obstruct OBOR and attempted to persuade U.S. allies and others to do the same. He advised cum pressured a number of countries to steer clear of China's Asian Infrastructure Investment Bank (AIIB), established in early 2016, that is a "backup" to OBOR. Obama perceived they challenged the World Bank, the Asian Development Bank and the International Monetary Fund—organizations the United States played a central role in creating and subsequently to a large degree controlled.

President Obama also found fault with OBOR as it countered his Asian pivot and its economic leg, the Trans-Pacific Partnership (TPP) agreement. The pivot and the TPP were anti-China and were conceived to stymie China's rise and weaken its influence in Asia where American influence was being challenged.

The Western media has long perceived that China's rise spells the waning of the Western, liberal global order. China does not adhere to the West's idea of what the world should be and it wants to create a Sino-centric world. OBOR epitomizes that.

Indeed OBOR will facilitate building China's "empire" and its destruction of the old, Western-built order. The Western media thus questions its purposes and criticizes it when it can. It ignores or plays down its huge contributions to global economic development, its helping developing countries and its abetting global progress overall.

NBC news described OBOR as having the potential to "upend" the world's geopolitics and economics. The *New York Times* wrote that "Mr. Xi" would create a "new kind of globalization" that will dispense with the aging Western-dominated system and "bring companies and countries into China's orbit."

Much of Europe followed the lead of the Western media, though the U.K., Germany, Poland and several other European countries are "joiners" in the belt linking Europe with Central Asia and China. European countries are envious of China's financial clout and are alarmed over the fact it has transformed the financial structure of the world from two polls, the Western poll comprised of Europe and the United States and the Eastern or Asian poll, to one centered in China.

So European countries carp that China building OBOR is ignoring human right and environmental standards. The European Union refused to endorse President Xi's statements made at the Forum meeting because it did not include commitments to social and environmental ideals and goals.

India and Japan are both fearful of China's rise and consider China a competitor for influence in Asia and beyond. Both have territorial disputes with China and both wish to contain China's growing economic and military clout.

India declined to send an official to the Forum meeting while newspapers in India called it China's "colonial enterprise."

In May India's Prime Minister Modi proposed establishing the Asia-Africa Growth Corridor (AAGC), with support from Japan, to contain Chinese influence on the African continent and enlarge their presence there.

An AAGA vision document was published at the time. The two governments proclaimed that their project would be cheaper and have a smaller carbon footprint than OBOR. Japan would contribute state-of-the art technology and know-how in building "quality infrastructure projects." India would contribute its expertise and experience in working with African countries.

Those supporting OBOR are as important as those who oppose and are arguable more numerous.

President Trump has taken a position diametrically opposed to President Obama's. He lauded OBOR and sent a delegation to the Forum. He declared that the United States wants to participate.

Matt Pottinger, the designated U.S. top delegate to the project, who is also a special assistant to Trump and the National Security Council's senior director for East Asia, declared that U.S. companies had "much to offer." GE, Caterpillar and a number of other huge US companies are planning to partake.

President Trump sees OBOR as an opportunity for American companies to make money and employ U.S. workers. Trump is a builder himself and sees the project as a positive influence in the world. He also wants better relations with China.

Russia is an enthusiastic participant. President Putin attended the Forum. Russia will benefit from the belt as it will give it access to important transportation routes and that will stimulate Russia's economy.

Russia, in addition, welcomes the global financial system's axis shifting ground, China buying more of Russia's natural resources and more inward investment.

Developing countries support OBOR. They are deeply impressed with the fact China has reduced poverty from 88 percent of its population 35 years ago to 2 percent now. They laud China's becoming the fastest growing major country in the world. They are grateful that China in the last decade plus has helped them grow economically with vast aid and investments. Africa, with China's financial help, has become the second leading area in the world in GDP growth in recent years.

Third World countries view OBOR as facilitating global trade that will benefit them while it relieves them of dependency ties with Western imperialist countries.

Countries along the belt or the road are especially happy about OBOR. It has put them on the geopolitical map. It has succored their economic development. It has afforded many of them modern infrastructure.

Pakistan, Sri Lanka, Bangladesh and Burma have in particular benefited economically and in other ways from China building billion dollar ports, accompanying roads, railroads, and pipelines along the maritime route. They speak highly of OBOR.

At the time China convened the forum observers predicted that if building OBOR stayed on track and does what China intends it would engender 2.5 trillion in trade among the involved countries. It would contribute immensely to global commerce and economic growth. It will be the project of the century.

It is likely OBOR will succeed given China's vast funding and its determination to see the project through, not to mention China's ability to build. Also the nations that support it, especially the United States, are more important than the ones that oppose it. Finally, Japan seems to have changed its position of late (due to the Trump administration endorsing it enthusiastically and Tokyo needing China's cooperation to deal with North Korea's threats).

ELEVEN

President Trump Dismisses Steve Bannon

The China Policy Factor

On August 18, 2017 President Trump "dismissed" his close friend and confidant, Steven Kevin Bannon, from his job as White House Chief Strategist. However, the official announcement was Bannon resigned. In any event it appeared Trump sought order among his White House advisors and Bannon was a major source of discord.

But policy was also involved. Bannon was a powerful ideologue and espoused a strong nationalist point of view on foreign policy issues. Trump was a proponent of bargaining and negotiating, which Bannon was not.

In particular the two were at odds over U.S. China policy.

Here are the details.

A year earlier, in August 2016, Donald Trump made Steve Bannon chief executive of his presidential campaign. Observers subsequently credited Bannon for Trump's victory by helping him win over conservatives and those unhappy with the direction America was going. They also cited Bannon's genius in formulating Trump's campaign tactics.

On foreign policy Bannon focused on the U.S. trade deficit, which he argued was profoundly hurting the U.S. economy and American workers. China was in his crosshairs. This was a winning issue in presidential campaigns as it had considerable resonance with American voters.

In November, following Trump's election victory, Bannon became chief strategist and senior counselor to the president-elect. After Donald Trump became President, Bannon kept his position on the White House team of advisors and also joined the National Security Council.

There soon developed serious friction between Bannon and other top White Officials. Bannon clashed with Chief of Staff Reince Priebus on a number of matters. When General John Kelly took over that position in early August he had serious gripes about Bannon. There were reports in the media and elsewhere of major discord among White House staff and that Bannon was the source. President Trump had to restore order out of the chaos.

This was the proximate or immediate cause for Bannon departure. Disagreements on policies, in particular U.S. China policy, were overshadowed for the moment by the personnel aspects of the event.

But policy tiffs were arguably salient and had implications for the Trump administration's efforts to manage global affairs. Relations with China took center stage.

Just two days before Bannon's departure, on August 16, he gave an interview with *The American Prospect* editor Robert Kuttner. Bannon said that the United States was engaged in an "economic war" with China. He further charged that America was losing the war.

Bannon went on to say that United States-China relations would hit an "inflection point" in ten years—from which "we will never be able to recover." He declared that "one of us is going to be a Hegemon in 25 or 30 years and it is gonna be them if we go down this path," referring to America's weak stance in allowing the trade deficit with China to persist.

Bannon further asserted that the North Korea crisis was "just a sideshow" and that China would do little to rein in Pyongyang.

Trump's White House Chief Strategist went on: Bannon stated that the United States is about to hit China hard over its unfair trade practices. He said specifically that the Trump administration would employ Section 301 of the 1974 Trade Act against China for its practice of using coercion to get technology from U.S. companies (by threatening to deny them access to the China market).

Finishing up, Bannon said: "We are going to run the tables on these guys," Bannon affirmed in any angry tone. He stated that the United States needed to be "maniacally focused" on the economic war with China.

At this point it became obvious that Bannon's ideas were very much at odds with President Trump's. The two were plainly not in sync on United States-China relations.

At the heart of their differences was the fact Trump was now president and had to make workable foreign policies. Campaigning was about rhetoric and ideology; now it was a different game.

Also Donald Trump was a transaction president. His approach to foreign relations was to negotiate and to do that he had to establish relationships with the leaders of important countries, understand them, and bargain (give and take) to resolve problems.

Henry Kissinger advised President Trump on China's importance of and how to deal with Chinese leaders. Former Treasury Secretary Hank Paulson counseled that the United States could not maintain the international financial system, deal with terrorism, control nuclear proliferation, and fix the global environment without working with China. Others told Trump the same thing.

President Trump put his negotiator strategy to work to repair United States-China relations, which were at a low point before Barack Obama left office. Specifically Trump displayed his approach to diplomacy during his first meeting with President Xi Jinping in April in Mar-a-Lago.

Trump calculated that China was the most important country in the world to the United States and that he needed China as a partner. He attained a foreign policy success.

President Trump also felt that President Xi realized that the trade deficit was unsustainable and if not reset would lead to greater problems, and was confident Xi would take steps to help mend it. But President Trump also knew that it could not be resolved in a short time; it had taken some time to grow into a serious problem and may take months or even years to fix it. (The U.S. trade deficit with China was $80 billion annually in 2001; in 2016 it was nearly $400 billion.)

President Xi responded: He pledged to buy American beef and allow U.S. financial companies to operate in China. Both were big items. Alas this constituted an important first step. America would also export liquid natural gas to China. This was another large items. They would cooperate on cyber issues. Much more was to come.

The deals were part of a 100-day period of negotiations. After the 100 days ended, the time frame was extended.

Shortly after the Mar-a-Lago meeting, in May, President Trump sent a representative to President Xi's Belt and Road (B&R) Initiative, formerly called OBOR, opening forum and gave his personal blessing to this gigantic project that emblemized China's rise and its growing role in the global financial system and the world economy.

President Trump's decision to do this was very significant.

The Obama administration had opposed the B&R Initiative and the banks China had created to finance it. President Obama advised, even pressured, U.S. allies not to join. The Western media expressed its resistance; it felt threatened by the project, which it perceived would spell the end of the Western, liberal global order. Western European countries didn't like the fact that human rights and governance were not made part of the project or that China negotiated bilaterally with the countries involved. Japan and India opposed China's B&R as it challenged their global influence.

President Xi needed America's help in getting the World Bank, the International Monetary Fund, the Asian Development Bank and other institutions involved. Trump would also influence other nations to join China's initiative. Japan soon changed its position.

President Trump wasn't threatened by China's growing dominance of global economic affairs. Alternatively, he thought he had a good bargaining position and should participate. Also he considered it was a positive force in Third World development.

Steve Bannon basically agreed with none of this.

President Trump subsequently "linked" talks on the United States-China trade dispute to China's help in dealing with the North Korea threat and U.S. efforts to denuclearize North Korea. China agreed to a United Nations sanctions proposal. China took other steps to restrain North Korea.

As a *quid pro quo* President Trump offered to not pursue regime change in North Korea or seek to unify Korea (with South Korea absorbing North Korea). He said he did not want to destroy North Korea; he only wanted to stop its building nuclear weapons and the missile delivery systems for them.

When President Trump perceived that China was not doing what he thought was enough he threatened to act alone and take (military) steps against North Korea. This was arguably a negotiating tactic. Trump hoped to get a more Chinese help. The fact he set no deadline seemed to indicate he sought further discussions with China.

President Trump's realist views influenced him in conducting U.S. foreign policy. So too did circumstances.

Enhancing U.S. military power became the key to President Trump's Asia policy. Specifically, Trump sought to restore the balance of power in East Asia that America had lost during previous administrations. This would enable him to negotiate with China from a position of strength.

Chinese leaders, in fact, conceded that the United States was way ahead of China in military power—even though China's military prowess was growing fast. America had the advantage of experience and a host of allies; China lacked both and this would likely last for some time. The fact that President Trump had increased U.S. spending on its military more than China seemed to add resonance to this reality.

Bannon didn't cotton to Trump's bargaining so much or what he thought was keeping America involved in useless wars.

At this time President Trump faced a special dilemma in Afghanistan. He had pledged get out of the war. It was America's longest war. It had taken its toll in lives and money. Americans wanted it over. But Trump did not wish to go down in history as losing a war or allowing Afghanistan to again become, more than it already was, a base for terrorism. He thus chose to increase U.S. troops in Afghanistan and remain in the conflict.

In so doing Donald Trump understood that expanding his military commitment to help the government of Afghanistan required money.

China was Afghanistan's bringer. Trump also grasped the fact that Pakistan was important to his efforts to win in Afghanistan. Again money was critical and China was Pakistan's biggest provider of foreign aid and investments.

Steve Bannon stuck to his view the United States should forthwith get out of the "prolonged and pointless" Afghanistan War and the United States should not depend on China for help.

President Trump faced still another problem that connected to China. He promised to fix America's infrastructure. But he realized he would likely face difficulties getting funding from Congress. So he looked to private investors. China might help.

Still another point of difference between President Trump and his chief advisor was the fact that Donald Trump liked and admired China. Trump had a fondness for China as witnessed by the fact his granddaughter was studying Chinese and speaking it daily and he boasted about it. He had used her to entertain and impress Chinese visitors.

From what he said both in public and in private Bannon didn't like China.

Adding to Trump's attraction to China he was acutely aware that the Western media disliked China as much as it abhorred him. In other words, Trump viewed the United States and China as having a common adversary. The Western media was doggedly unfair to both and showed bias (often extreme) in reporting on them.

Not coincidently Bannon's news outlet, Brietbart, had long expressed dislike of China and recommended a hostile policy toward China, much as the liberal Western media did.

The bottom line was that President Trump espoused negotiating to get things done while he was optimistic about United States-China relations. Steve Bannon espoused a zero sum perception of United States-China relations and saw China very differently.

This goes far to explain Trump seeing Bannon's exit from the White House team of advisors.

TWELVE

The U.S. Liberal Media's Treatment of President Trump's Asia Trip Versus Asian Reporting

On November 3, 2017, U.S. President Donald J. Trump embarked on his first official trip to Asia. This was his longest foreign trip as president. It was arguably his most important one.

President Trump, accompanied by the First Lady, first stopped in Hawaii. This was the natural launching point for the Asia tour. It signaled that the United States is a nation with links to the Pacific that it plans to keep.

The rest of his schedule was: Japan on November 5, South Korea on November 7, China on the 8th, Vietnam on the 10th and the Philippines on November 12. On all of his stops he met heads-of-state and other dignitaries and engaged in negotiations on critical policy issues.

Foremost on the president's agenda was dealing with the North Korea threat and fixing the U.S. trade deficit (bigger in Asia than elsewhere). President Trump also sought to reaffirm U.S. commitments to Asia/Pacific countries, promote America's defense ties with the nations in the region, establish rapport with important regional organizations in Southeast Asia, and more.

The American mainstream or liberal media, almost in unison, put a negative spin on President Trump's trip. They pooh-poohed any notion of it being a success or that Trump made a good impression on Asian leaders and the peoples of the Asian countries he visited, or even that he advanced U.S. national interests.

The *Washington Post* portrayed President Trump's Asia sojourn as "successful only in his mind and full of gaffes even though it was highly choreographed." The *Post* reported Trump made no mention of democracy or human rights and that he outraged Americans with his meeting with Russian President Vladimir Putin. Also Trump, according to the "paper of record," ignored questions about the depletion of personnel in the Department of State and its diminished role during the trip.

The *New York Times* carried stories about China's return to a tough authoritarian system that was the prelude cum setting to President Trump's visit. An article penned by Susan Rice, once President Obama's national security advisor, read that the trip "left the United States more isolated and in retreat, handing leadership of the newly christened 'Indo-Pacific' to China on a silver platter."

USA Today reported that President Trump likes Asia because he idolizes the authoritarian strongmen there and he is a wannabe despot. Further the paper opined that Trump is "the kind of demagogue that the founding fathers warned of" and that "American democracy is now under threat."

CNN declared that President Trump failed to fix U.S. trade problems with Asian countries as witnessed by 11 nations that were part of the Trans-Pacific Partnership agreement (that Trump had cancelled) meeting to renew the agreement without the United States. Further, Trump went back on several campaign promises about reversing the trade deficit with China.

CNBC declared Trump "begged for war" with North Korea during his trip to Asia, characterizing him a warmonger.

NBC News explained the reason for the trip was President Trump wanting to avoid or dodge nettlesome questions that he faced at home.

Associated Press replayed Democratic Party Senate Majority leader Chuck Schumer's comment that Trump's trip was a "colossal failure" and a "big embarrassment" to the United States.

Time magazine's cover story was about Trump's trip being a big, smart and sensational victory for China. The cover of the magazine displayed prominently the words "China won" in English and in Chinese. *Time* also carried details of Trump's "awkward handshakes" with Asian leaders and his deliberately eschewing any talks about human rights.

The *Economist* magazine, a British publication with more readers in the United States than the U.K, and conservative but fervently anti-Trump, reported that President Trump's trip provided clear evidence America's global influence has dwindled.

The Asian media's account of President Trump's trip stood in stark contrast to the U.S. mainstream media's reporting. It was largely positive and laudatory of the U.S. president.

The *Japan Times*, Japan's main English newspaper, referred to the visit as "tremendously successful." Other Japanese media sources reported smooth talks on trade, President Trump and Prime Minister Abe and other leaders' great relationships, and Japan heartily supporting President Trump's stance toward North Korea.

Asahi Shimbun, one of Japan's largest Japanese-language newspapers, applauded President Trump's appreciation of Japan's importance as a U.S. ally and his rapport with the U.S. and Japanese militaries.

The Japanese press also described at length and in positive terms President Trump's talks with Japanese families whose members had been kidnapped by North Korean agents and Trump meeting with Japan's Emperor.

While in South Korea, the country's largest newspaper, *Chosun Ilbo*, lauded President Trump's tough position toward North Korea mentioning specifically his "moral case" against Kim Jong-Un. Another leading paper, *Joongang Ilbo*, called Trump's speech to the National Assembly "eloquent"—noting there were 22 rounds of applause and two standing ovations during the speech.

The South Korean media also cited "flexibility" on President Trump's part toward reaching a diplomatic solution to North Korea's nuclear weapons and missile tests and its war threats. News outlets praised Trump's "Reaganesque efforts" to secure peace through strength.

South Korean reporters even wrote about President Moon working with President Trump to bolster the nation's self-defense capabilities, mentioning specifically South Korea's plans to acquire the most advanced U.S. surveillance equipment and possibly a U.S. nuclear-powered submarine.

During his visit to China the *China Daily* described President Trump as "fully capable of anchoring United States-China relations." The paper also cited the "precious progress" made in Sino-United States business. Other papers used the words "terrific" and "tremendous" to depict President Trump's diplomatic performance.

Global Times, the main English-language paper that carries important news about foreign relations and which has sometimes been critical of President Trump, called his visit "successful and historic." One reporter for the *Times* wrote that President Xi and President Trump had "reached a consensus on advancing bilateral ties to the next phase."

Global Times also reported progress on the issues President Trump said were his foremost goals on his trip. Citing a Ministry of Foreign Affairs spokesperson it wrote that there was agreement on the "complete, verifiable and irreversible denuclearization" of the Korean Peninsula and the two countries, China and the United States, would not recognize North Korea as a nuclear power.

The paper's reporters also penned articles on resolving the trade imbalance citing "furthering mutual beneficial cooperation" and "constructing a bigger cake." They cited the $253.5 billion in Chinese pledges to buy American products as "building a wide foundation."

Global Times even quoted top Chinese officials saying China was not planning to take advantage of the Trump administration as the U.S. media had suggested, as China would not forcefully influence the international division of labor.

Netizens in China showed an unprecedented interest in President Trump and the First Lady; millions made laudatory comments about them. Many referred to President Trump as a "hero" and as a "savior." Millions more wrote about President Trump and the First Lady being given a state dinner in the Forbidden City noting it was a first for an American president and the first for a foreign head-of-state since the establishment of the People's Republic of China in 1949.

While visiting Vietnam, Radio Voice of Vietnam reported Donald Trump was the first U.S. president ever to visit Vietnam during his initial year in office. The radio station also praised President Trump's decision to attend the APEC Economic Leaders' Meeting while there, saying it demonstrated his commitment to strengthening U.S. relations with Vietnam and the region.

Vietnam's media also reported that its government was committed to the "Maximum Pressure Campaign" to denuclearize North Korea, that Vietnam and the United States had concluded a Three Year Plan of Action for Defense Cooperation to increase joint naval activities, the United States transferred a Coast Guard cutter to the Vietnamese Navy, a U.S. aircraft carrier would visit Vietnam in 2018, that the two countries reaffirmed their commitments to freedom of navigation, overflight and commerce in the South China Sea and commercial agreements reached that included $10 billion in U.S. content. President Trump and Vietnamese leaders also spoke of the importance of promoting human rights.

Vietnam's media, of course, played up the importance of President Trump's visit and the glamor of state dinners and other social events America's president and First Lady attended.

In the Philippines the media gave President Trump a hearty welcome. The *Philippine Star*, called a paper of record, mentioned that the two countries' presidents held mutually supportive talks on ridding ISIS-inspired terrorists from the Philippines, the strategic importance of the Philippines to the United States, and future United States-ASEAN maritime exercises. President Duterte backed President Trump's call for a unified tough stance to deal with North Korea's nuclear arms and missile threats.

Philippine newspapers reported extensively on President Trump's participation in the 50th anniversary of ASEAN and the 40th ASEAN-United States Commemorative Summit while underscoring the "grace" of President Trump's presence. They also expressed appreciation for Trump extending his visit in the Philippines by one day.

The Vietnamese and the Philippine press both cited the importance of the Trump administration increasing U.S. defense spending that would include expanding the American naval presence in the area to preserve U.S. influence and prevent any outside power from gaining military dominance.

How does one explain the utter disconnect between the U.S. mainstream media's reporting on the Trump visit and that provided by the local Asian media?

The U.S. media is by culture, ideology and its preference for political parties and their candidates liberal to very liberal. They championed Hillary Clinton for president by a large margin, giving donations to the Democratic Party and the Clinton campaign and voting for her by an unprecedented 90-some percent. In 2016 they, with great enthusiasm, wanted and expected her to win and become the next U.S. president.

They reviled Donald Trump. They were shocked by his victory and didn't accept it. They were subsequently obsessed with seeing him fail or removing him from office somehow, by hook or by crook. They were literally overcome with hate. They suffered from what many called the "Trump derangement syndrome."

Their reporting was so affected. The liberal mainstream media in the United States spun their stories in a negative fashion on virtually everything related to President Trump. They wanted to discredit him and his administration. This became a mission of their profession.

Also the U.S. liberal media view Asia and Asians as traditional cum conservative. Indeed this fits. Also conservatives in the United States, whom the mainstream media dislike intensely, had long had an affinity toward Asia; liberals had a liking and an attraction for Europe. Worsening this situation is the fact that Asia was becoming the center of gravity of global economic growth and progress while Europe was heading toward irrelevance due to its economic sclerosis made worse by demographic and political trends.

Many in the U.S. media, via their positions on various issues, reveal that they deride the people and the countries of the Asia-Pacific region. In the United States, liberal Hollywood portrays Asians in movies and on television with negative stereotypes or shuns them. (Asians do not appear in U.S. movies or on television very often in contrast to other minorities.) Liberals supported racial policies in selecting out Asians from admission to America's best colleges and universities. They favor immigrants from other areas of the world.

The U.S. liberal media's ill feelings toward China were especially pronounced. China is the dominant country in Asia and its phenomenal rise in economic, political and military power enable it to challenge the Western-built liberal world order. The U.S. mainstream media dread prospects of China realizing its dream of establishing its world order.

The China challenge cum threat was even more poignant in the wake of the just finished Chinese Communist Party's 19th Congress. At that meeting President Xi Jinping promoted China's role in building a new world order, one that would replace the old and out-of-date Western liberal world order.

Whose interpretations of President Trump's visit to Asia is right—the U.S. liberal media or the news organizations in the Asian countries the president visited?

The fact the U.S. media is not in good standing with the population of the United States as reflected in various opinion polls (that rate them very low and declining, especially the national media) is telling. It suggests the public views them as biased and closed minded. So does the fact many liberal newspapers and television stations in the United States are losing readers and viewers.

This is not the case in Asia. It is also noteworthy, even astounding, that the five Asian countries President Trump visited are profoundly dissimilar in terms of history, culture, language, politics and policies. Yet all reported, in contrast to the U.S. mainstream media, Trump's visit was successful and productive.

Another takeaway is that in United States the Asian media was quoted infrequently and thus different perspectives on President Trump's trip were not very available. This was also noticeable in using Internet searches articles and in the social media. The consequence of all of this was that the U.S. news reporting on the trip was less diverse and less informative.

Finally, the conclusion is inescapable that the media in most Asian countries have become more objective and more professional. The opposite has happened in the United States.

THIRTEEN

Explaining the Recent Tension in United States-China Relations

In the early months of 2018 United States-China relations sunk to a state somewhere between frosty and hostile. This marked a transformative change since President Trump visited China in November 2017.

There were several reasons for this.

The simple explanation is that President Trump got China to promise to fix the trade deficit and help the United States apply sanctions on North Korea to force Kim Jung Un to negotiate ending his nuclear weapons and missile programs. But Trump soon became dismayed with the results of both.

Instead of the U.S. trade deficit decreasing it increased. This was partly a product of the U.S. economy improving and thus stimulating America's demand for more Chinese products. It was also the result of Chinese leaders assuming that this was a long-term goal and acting on it quickly and energetically contradicted dealing with economic problems at home especially unemployment in China.

Chinese leaders no doubt also coupled fixing the trade deficit with solving the North Korea problem and reckoned helping the U.S. deal with North Korea meant they did not have to treat the trade deficit as an urgent problem. Anyway, they wanted to proceed cautiously on North Korea as they did not want to cause the regime there to implode; it was evident to China that Kim Jung-un faced problems at home in meeting U.S. demands.

In any event, President Trump was embarrassed cum angry that the trade deficit grew. It also became glaringly evident that China's "Made in China 2025" strategy launched in 2015 was on a collision course with President Trump's "Make America Great Again" policy. The former would make China the foremost country in the world in advanced manufacturing and much more. Trump wanted to fix America's economy and restore America's global leadership in high tech and a lot more. Thus the conflict with China grew.

Trump's chosen strategy was to place tariffs on Chinese goods entering the United States knowing China depended more on exports than the United States. He also understood the deficit was the cause of factories closing in the United States, the loss of jobs and a huge and dangerous debt and using shock treatment was the way to successful negotiations.

Thus, in March 2018 the Trump administration announced tariffs on $60 billion of Chinese imports. At the time Trump cited the results of a Section 301 (of the Trade Act of 1974) investigation into China's unfair trade practices: disregard for rules on intellectual property, discrimination against foreign (e.g. American) firms, industrial policies that favored Chinese companies.

The Section 301 report also named a Chinese government initiative as emblematic of China's bad behavior: Made in China 2025.

Trump's tariffs had a significant impact on China, both economically and politically.

Growth of China's GDP slowed. Its stock market sputtered. There was a slowdown in construction. Productivity declined. There were increasing worries about its domestic debt (now said to be 250 percent of GDP). The Yuan fell and this trammeled China's influence in international finance.

Further, the Chinese government's options in controlling the economy seemed to be in question. A recent $600 billion stimulus package created problems in the private sector and did not now seem a good idea.

Political problems followed the negative economic news.

President Trump criticized China openly for the trade deficit and spoke of more, perhaps endless, tariffs.

Chinese leaders felt compelled to answer tit for tat. China placed tariffs on U.S. products exported to China. Fees on some items such as soybeans were aimed at one of Trump's favorite voting constituencies. Meanwhile China's media accused President Trump of launching a trade war.

China's actions had an impact on the U.S. economy and American politics. In addition, it caused U.S. friends and allies to warn President Trump he was causing a risk to world trade and what he was doing was wrong.

There was another variable affecting United States-China relations: neither the media nor pundits linked to domestic politics and did not often discuss in this context. That is that the United States was in an election campaign mode.

During recent election campaigns China has always been an issue. American politicians have found it convenient to portray China as a bogyman. China's rise is a challenge to the United States. Politicians also love scapegoats and during election campaigns China has been a favorite.

During the heat of the 1980 presidential election campaign Ronald Reagan castigated President Jimmy Carter for his weak and wrong-headed diplomatic recognition of "Communist China"—which Reagan said Carter did for political reasons notably his low opinion poll numbers. He lauded the Taiwan Relations Act that "corrected Carter's mistakes."

Reagan asserted he "would not betray friends and allies." He even said on several occasions during the campaign he would support reestablishing diplomatic ties with Taiwan.

After the election the Reagan administration cemented a better working relationship with China than had ever been the case before. U.S. military officers engaged with their counterparts for the first time. U.S. defense and intelligence agencies worked closely with China on such issues as the Afghanistan war. Reagan approved the sale of dual-use high tech items to China. U.S. Navy ships made their first visits to Chinese ports.

Reagan never spoke again about restoring formal ties with Taiwan.

In 1992 candidate Bill Clinton blasted President George H.W. Bush for "coddling dictators" in China citing Tiananmen Square and mentioning specifically Bush's "sending a secret emissary to toast those who crushed democracy in China."

But as President Clinton de-linked most-favored-nation trade status for China from the human rights issues. He said it was "time to take a new path." Clinton later moved to establish a United States-China strategic partnership and invited President President Jiang Zemin to Washington for an official state visit—the first in twelve years. He then travelled to China for an unprecedented ten-day summit.

During the 2000 campaign George W. Bush excoriated President Clinton for his big "departure" on China policy from the campaign to governing. Specifically, he stated: "China is a competitor, not a strategic partner."

In office Bush didn't talk of competitor and instead spoke of cooperation with China.

Barack Obama, during the 2008 presidential election campaign criticized the $1 trillion debt owed to China and called China a "currency manipulator." He rebuked China for violations of human rights and intellectual property rules.

Once president, Obama talked about "continuity" in U.S. China policy and used terms such as "positive cooperative" and "comprehensive" to describe United States-China relations.

The election this November is only a mid-term and it should not be so important or so much about foreign policy; but for a number of reasons, it is.

First, the liberal Western media is on a tear against China. Its anti-China obsession is almost as strong as its anti-Trump syndrome. China is condemned because it is destroying the liberal world order and is substituting its own for it. China's "order," the media charge, is not democratic, not egalitarian, not focused on international law, etc.,

The "Beijing consensus" (China's much better economic performance than the Western democracies, when democracy was suppose to facilitate economic growth, while it worked miracles in reducing poverty and maintaining social order and progress) it challenged democracy on a worldwide scale.

China's rise is thus a trend that needs to be reversed, said the liberal media.

Second, the Democratic Party needed some fungible election issues. That Russia reportedly gave Trump the election win in 2016 had grown shopworn and lacked credibility. Democratic Party strategists were in search of a topic to counter Trump's record and his success in "making America great again."

The U.S. media and academe making China a "whipping boy" and portraying it as a menace to America was easy because Americans' knowledge of China was superficial and was mainly provided by liberal hate-China news outlets. Also U.S. China scholars were mostly on board and loved to write about pollution, corruption, real estate bubbles, etc. in China and ignore China's being the foremost nation in the world in green energy and its helping alleviate global poverty and economic growth as no country ever has.

It was also telling that the United States sends to China less than 1 percent of the students China sends to the United States. The number is about the same as U.S. students studying in Ireland. Americans did not understand China.

Alas, condemning China was thus something for Democrats to grasp onto. The media and academe laid the groundwork. Opinion polls showed the number of Americans that believe China is a threat had tripled in the last year.

Third, Democrats sorely needed to rationalize their hardly veiled racism against Asians, especially Chinese, via their support for affirmative action especially as it its manifest in discrimination against Asians in admission to America's best colleges and universities.

Chinese in American recently underscored this issue by suing Harvard University for its racially biased admissions policies.

Meanwhile, recent opinion polls taken of Chinese in the United States show that they feel they are discriminated against in Boston more than any other American city. This is because of the numerous top universities there that deny equal or fair entrance to Chinese. Chinese have even been heard saying, "liberals hate Chinese" because they are conservative in their views and dislike big government, high taxes, etc.

The upshot is President Trump needs a fight with China over trade lest the Democrats capture and fully exploit the anti-China issue during the election campaign.

In fact, he may even diffuse the anti-China rage since the left cannot agree with Trump on anything.

After the election one can expect President Trump as other presidents before him will restore good relations with China. He still has a lot of good will in China. Also Chinese leaders realize that the United States cannot sustain the current trade imbalance or the debt it generates.

Finally, the nexus of good United States-China relations is a *sine qua non* to maintain a stable financial world system, control nuclear proliferation, deal with the global environment, etc. Both President Trump and Chinese leaders know this.

FOURTEEN

The U.S. Trade Deficit with China

Facing Dilemmas

A learned scholar once proclaimed: "Economic issues are almost always also political issues." He might have added that the debate about America's trade deficit with China is this in spades.

The U.S. trade deficit with China, in fact, is so serious it imperils relations between the two major world powers and may start a trade war that affects the entire planet.

The magnitude of the deficit tells part of the story. In 2017, America's trade deficit totaled a whopping $566 billion—the world's largest. America's trade deficit with China was $375 billion. This shortfall with China eclipsed the U.S. deficit with any other country: $71 billion with Mexico $69 billion with Japan, $65 billion with Germany. This situation was obviously unsustainable. It also invited demagoguery,

The facts are: Coinciding with the trade deficit America lost many of its industries. Manufacturing jobs declined by 34 percent from 1998 to 2010 and continued to disappear after that. The aftereffects included welfare payments that ballooned and unemployment benefits that grew (many of which were turned into long-term disabilities during the Obama years to keep the unemployment rate from looking even worse). Lost industries also meant America could not afford so much research and R& D was rendered much less efficient since there were fewer places to test it.

Taxes increased, as did the U.S. debt. The U.S. budget line item for interest on the national debt crowded out other items. The government's help to business declined (including subsidizes which all governments do). Exports fell. Countries, i.e., China, with trade and budget surpluses faced the opposite situation. China could afford more money for R&D to help its promising industries and companies.

Since China invested much of the funds gained from its trade surplus with the United States in America, the U.S. debt to China grew, to $1.17 trillion as of January 2018, or 19 percent of the public U.S. debt owned by foreigners. If China were to cash in much of this it would cause interest rates in the United States to spike and jolt the housing market. That might set off a recession that would spread around the world.

Meanwhile China continued using its trade surplus with America to buy U.S. companies and invest in others. This became a serious problem because many of the companies China bought were involved in high tech.

Free trade is supposed to resolve this situation. But it is an ideal; in reality it is more a cliché than a policy that is practiced. Currency devaluations, the theory holds, would resolve a trade imbalance. But using this mechanism causes others to employ it too in order to remain competitive; it thus invites currency wars. Anyway the U.S. dollar is a global tender and must remain stable and strong for the global financial system to work. A strong currency is also necessary if the United States is to remain a global superpower, as it so desires.

Hence the global financial system is not working. Yet the politicians still speak of free trade as if it is desirable and will fix all problems.

Who is to blame for this situation? Those quick to judge say it is China cheating in trade. This is the bromide of the Western mainstream media that despises China because it is destroying the liberal world order and supplanting it with its own. Anyway politicians seek scapegoats.

So, China is said to be protectionist. According to the narrative, it undervalues its currency (so that it can sell more goods) and steals intellectual property from foreign enterprises (so it can move up the innovation curve quickly and at little expense).

But are these charges true? If they are, are they meaningful?

China is, of course, protectionist. But so are most nations. China's protectionism is not seriously different. In fact, China's trade surplus got worse after it joined the World Trade Organization, which is the overseer of global trade. China's protectionism cum mercantilism is more destabilizing because China's economy is larger. Is it reasonable China be judged by how big its economy is?

China's currency, it is said, is undervalued. But some say it is overvalued. If China wants to be a bigger player in global finance, as its critics say, and fear, its currency should be overvalued. But the Chinaphobes oppose China's dominance in international economic affairs! Anyway a number of top economists say its currency valuation is not an important factor in explaining the U.S. trade deficit with China.

Is China pinching intellectual property? The answer is yes; but there is more to say than that. Most nations do this. Again it is a matter of China's size. Also China is more successful at it than most because it presents it as a bargain—technology for access to the huge and growing China market. U.S. companies are not forced to give up their technology; they do so to attain quick profits to satisfy their stockholders.

In any case, China is putting more money and resources into advancing its technology (around 18 percent annual increases in R&D spending compared to the United States approximately 3 percent). As a result it is registering more patents each year and is making more technological breakthroughs than the United States. Thus American companies are eyeing China's technology and it will not be too long before the technology-taking situation is reversed.

Given there are no real solutions to be found or reasonable charges against China, one might conjecture that the answers to the problem lie with what the United States is not doing right and what it might do to fix its trade deficit. The obvious best solution to the problem is for the United States to export more to China. (Blocking imports from China will be badly inflationary and runs the danger of engendering a trade war.)

Two obstacles that are of the upmost importance in making it possible for the United States to export more to China are high taxes (U.S. corporate taxes have been among the highest in the world) and burdensome regulations that many business leaders say are a worse hindrance.

President Trump has taken meaningful actions to rectify both. And his efforts have had a major impact. GDP growth, investments, and employment are all up. But the advantage is still with China. Can he do more? Doubtful; the politicians stand in his way.

In looking for other solutions Trump and his advisors need to consider the United States needs to reduce its huge and smothering debt. In 2017 the federal government took in $3.3 trillion in taxes. Yet spending exceeded that by $665 billion. The cause is members of Congress who pander for votes by offering government goodies. That is the way America's mass democracy works these days: politicians offer benefits to the poor for votes knowing they will be out of office before the bills comes due.

Even President Trump's recent budget is full of this kind of spending. Trump had to compromise to get other things he wanted.

The two biggest spending items are health care and social security. Health care costs in the United States are almost the highest in the world and are expected to increase by 6 percent annually for at least a decade. Social security expenditures will increase fast as a result of aging and more people retiring. Will either be fixed, or will the politicians simply kick the can down the road?

The federal government's budget also includes a line item for interest payments amounting to 7 percent of total spending. Some projections are that this will more than double in five years at which time the amount needed for interest payments will exceed spending on national defense.

Meanwhile this will affect everything else in the budget. Especially important in terms of the question at hand, it takes away money for improving America's infrastructure that has been allowed to become dilapidated under Trump's predecessors and reduces spending on R&D, upon which product advances depend (i.e., keeping up with the innovation curve).

Looking ahead entitlements and the interests on the debt together will consume one hundred percent of taxes paid now in less than a decade. Still politicians don't offer any meaningful answers. The political left wants more taxes to pay for these things, but they don't think of the consequences.

There are also many costs outside the budget and they are a big drag on business, notably exports. Again the solutions to trammeling these expenditures are political and nothing is happening to remedy the situation.

The cost of lawyers in the United States is an enormous burden on doing business. Liability costs as a percentage of the gross domestic product are two and one half times the average of countries in the Eurozone. They are many fold China's.

Little to nothing is being done to change this. It is no wonder many say the United States is a "nation of lawyers" and note that law is the main, cum "required," background of members of Congress. This is seldom the training of high officials in China. Meeting growing legal requirements not only are costly but also results in long delays in getting things done.

Not unrelated to this problem, the U.S. criminal justice and penal systems are horrendously expensive. Since 1980 this budget item has grown by 4.5 fold and employs 2.2 million people—higher per the total population than any other OECD country and four times the world average. The usual figure cited for incarcerating criminals is $80 billion per year.

Some researchers, however, say the cost of incarceration is only one-tenth of the total "social cost" of crime, that includes damage done to families and communities, The gross costs the data show amount to six percent of the gross domestic product or over $1 trillion a year.

Related to this problem is America's substance abuse crisis. The opioid crisis has cost a reported $1 trillion since 2001 and is climbing. This does not include other illegal drugs.

The expense of illegal immigrants in the United States is still another huge burden. It is estimated the expenditures by government (state, local and federal) each year totals annually more than $134 billion. Since the taxes they pay amount to less than $18 billion the shortfall is $116 billion a year.

This figure is no doubt low, as it does not count the secondary costs or future expenditures.

The costs of these items to China are markedly less. For example, China has 1.7 million incarcerated people, just over half the United States even though China's population is more than four fold America's. The cost per prisoner is much less in China; China spends $22,000 per prisoner annually. California spends $75,000. New York City spends over $150,000. Yet the recidivism rate in China is much lower.

China has 300,000 lawyers (which arguably may not be enough); but the United States has 1.34 million (which according to a host of measures is way too many). In fact, many analysts see lawyers in the United States as a pernicious form of corruption.

The drug problem in China is tiny compared to the United States. Almost in unison citizens in China (as in most Asian countries) say that illegal drug peddlers should be executed and if you do not believe that you hate your children and grandchildren. Many in the United States consider selling drugs a non-violent crime and thus not serious.

The cost of illegal immigrants in China is miniscule. China has accepted more than a million refuges from Vietnam. They were found jobs. China has foreign workers; but since China is not a welfare state they have not become a cost to taxpayers. Currently only immigrants that have skills are admitted. The United States almost alone in the world accepts immigrants indiscriminately.

The list goes on.

The explanation for this situation is easy looking back in time a bit. The United States used to have a trade surplus with China), when China was a socialist (or communist) country and America was a capitalist country. Now that is reversed (judging from the percentage of the economy that is in the public sector and controlled by self-serving politicians).

Looking at the variances between the United States and China from a different angle, but one that also explains why the United States is not competing, Wendy Wang of the Institute for Family Studies notes one big difference between the two countries is what she calls "the sequence": education, work, marriage, children in that order. In China less than 4 percent of children are born out of wedlock. In the United States it is 40 percent (70 percent plus for blacks).

This explains a lot. For millennials who marry before having children the probability of being in poverty (and usually dependent on social welfare and unproductive) is 60 percent higher; for those out of sequence on three items it is 90 percent more.

The "social" and "extra" financial costs the United States bears means its tax burden is higher and its business less competitive. This impedes product improvement. It slows exports.

Managed trade may fix this. Free trade will not; in fact, it makes it permanent thanks to America's political class.

FIFTEEN

The Worsening U.S. Trade Deficit with China

Heading for a Trade War?

As of late 2017 and early 2018, the U.S. trade balance with China, which was supposed to improve after visits by President Xi Jinping to Mar-a-Lago, Florida in April 2017 and President Trump's Asia trip in November that included an important stop in China, had not happened.

During both meetings critical commercial deals were struck.

Yet, the United States-China trade ledger now has even more red ink for America.

The U.S. trade deficit rose 12 percent in 2017 to $566 billion—constituting the biggest gap in imports and exports since 2008. A shortfall in U.S. exports to China versus imports from China accounted for nearly half of that. Worse, the trade deficit with China had risen by 8 percent since Donald Trump had become president.

In response Trump administration officials went on the offensive. Some blamed and berated China. President Trump ordered tariffs on solar panels. He also charged China with violating intellectual property rights rules while slamming China for aggressively demanding U.S. companies surrender their technology to China in exchange for access to China's huge and expanding market—a demand they usually do not refuse. Trump people labeled this an unfair trade practice.

Some Trump supporters in the meantime complain he has failed to fulfill his campaign promises to label China a currency manipulator and do something more drastic about the trade imbalance such as applying a 45 percent punitive tariff on Chinese imports.

In January 2018 President Trump addressed the renowned World Economic Forum annual meeting in Davos, Switzerland. There he promised to reform the international trading system so that it "rewards those who play by the rules." Some took that to be a slap at China; others said Trump was starting a trade war. Critics in the liberal media said his actions on solar panels and refrigerators would start a "cycle of unilateral moves" against free trade that would become contagious.

At nearly the same time U.S. Secretary of the Treasury Steven Mnuchin spoke in positive terms of a U.S. devaluation of the dollar (to help fix the trade deficit) and the dollar quickly fell. Critics began to talk of Trump provoking a currency war that would broaden into something worse.

Meanwhile there were heard repeated cries from the anti-Trump liberal Western media that Trump was a protectionist and would cause a trade war that might even lead to a war with weapons of mass destruction.

Where is the United States-China trade relationship going? What is the truth in all of this?

The answers are: Much of what was reported about President Trump recklessly starting a trade war and his actions against China that were front and center, were either untrue or were grossly exaggerated. There were also extenuating circumstances and events.

First, U.S. exports rose overall in 2017 (Trump's first year in office) by 5.5 percent. In December U.S. external sales jumped by the fastest pace ever for one month. However, imports rose by 6.7 percent, the highest increase since 2011 and to a record level.

So much for Trump being a protectionist who would constrict foreign trade.

Second, President Trump immediately talked down (even contradicted his Treasury Secretary) the so-called plan to devalue the dollar. After a reaction in the stock market and some disquiet abroad, calm quickly returned. Subsequently, little was heard about this.

Third, the trade deficit with China was caused in large measure by good economic news in the United States. Trump's deft stewardship of the U.S. economy spearheaded by the tax reform package stimulated growth and with it a big spike in consumer spending. Americans were buying more products made overseas (including China). In the meantime China's economy perked up and with that its exports increased.

It is, of course, ironic that good economic news begat bad economic news; but that is sometimes how things are.

Fourth, there was another important issue before the Trump administration that affected talks and actions on United States-China trade: the North Korea nuclear threat. It was the belief that China's cooperation was essential in helping Washington deal with this problem. Indeed China had considerable leverage; and China and the United States were generally on the same page (on nuclear proliferation and more). So good news was expected on this issue.

But the North Korean regime was always a tough one for China to deal with. Also Chinese leaders did not want to see a collapse of the government and Korea's reunification. Secretary of State Tillerson said this was also U.S. policy, but Chinese officials were hesitant to assume, at least without some pause, this was true. Anyway the process of using sanctions on North Korea was likely to be an extended one.

In short, the North Korea problem diverted American policy-makers' attention away from the trade deficit. Likewise for Chinese leaders.

Fifth, President Xi made promises when he visited Mar-a-Lago in April 2017 and again when President Trump visited China the following November to cut the trade deficit. During the first meeting Xi pledged to open China's financial services market to American companies and import American beef, plus he offered a hundred days of further talks to do more to fix the problem. During the second meet President Xi agreed to purchase a whopping $253.4 billion worth of American products.

Were President Xi's pledges insincere?

No! In both cases it would take time to realize results from the deals. Getting into China's financial services market would require American companies to make plans that would take months before results would be seen. The latter deal included memoranda of understanding that would entail further negotiations. Part of the deal included buying 300 planes from Boeing; most of that promise would take years to fulfill since Boeing already had a large number of orders to fill.

Thus, for the United States to accrue benefits from these promises is something that will happen mainly in the future, not the present. Yet it is not likely the promises will not be kept.

Indicating President Xi considers reducing China's large trade surplus with the United States a top priority, he is reported to have pulled a trusted ally, Wang Qishan (known as the "fireman" for his skill in handling emergencies) from mandatory retirement to deal with United States-China relations. Further, just days earlier President Xi was reported sending his top economic policymaker, Liu He, to Washington to discuss trade.

Sixth, U.S. businesses are optimistic about economic relations with China as shown in a recent survey taken by the American Chamber of Commerce in China. Of the 411 members queried 46 percent said they believed China was committed to further opening up, compared to 34 percent that voiced that opinion a year earlier. A significant 64 percent reported their revenues were up in 2017; 55 percent had said that in 2016. Most reported that profits were up. Three quarter said they planned to increase investments in China.

This would not be the case if American business leaders operating in China expected a crisis leading to a trade war.

Seventh, and very important to understanding the current situation, espousing anti-China sentiment and expressing it in public and to the media is a good election tactic and America is already in an election mode. Moreover, most consider the November 2018 election to be a critical one. The Democratic Party was expected to capture a majority in the House of Representatives; in fact the average gain for the party out of power in an off-year election is 25 seats. If the Democrats gained that number of seats plus one it will be in the majority and would be able to impeach President Trump in 2019 as they have been anxious to do (though they would be unlikely to convict him in the Senate).

Thus criticism of China over the trade deficit is part of the campaign narrative and making China a scapegoat for things going wrong in America is old hat. When George Bush I ran for president he tried to cover up his good relationship with China and sold fighter aircraft to Taiwan. Bill Clinton castigated China for human rights abuses and for the trade deficit and castigated Bush for his close ties with China. When George Bush II ran he declared he would do "whatever it took" to help Taiwan. Meanwhile, his opponents vilified China on several fronts.

This being the case, during this campaign period candidates are certain to employ hostile rhetoric toward China. It will come from both liberal and conservative candidates. It has already started. After the election it is to be expected this will dissipate and the relationship will return to normal. Both United States and Chinese leaders understand this.

Given all of this, the current trade spat between the United States and China should not be seen as leading to something catastrophic. United States-China relations are generally good, much better than during the later years of the Obama administration. Both sides fully realize that to maintain a stable international financial regime, prevent nuclear proliferation, protect the global environment and much more, cordial, workable United States-China relations must be maintained.

SIXTEEN

The Top Two Targets of Western Liberal Media Bias

President Donald Trump and China

Proof can be heard and seen almost daily of Western liberal media bias against U.S. President Donald J. Trump and contemporary China. They are regarded as foes to discredit, embarrass, undermine, and more. The two are the foremost targets of the liberal Western media unfairness and ill will like no others.

This generates questions about how to view politics in the two countries, the critically important United States-China relationship, and the need for stability in global affairs. There is a lot at stake.

The details are instructive.

President Donald J. Trump is the primary bull's eye of liberal media's attacks. When did this begin? Why? How is it manifested?

This started when Donald Trump entered the race for president. The U.S. mainstream media at first tried to ignore him. Then, as he performed well during the campaign they came to fear and loathe him. This increased exponentially when he won the Republican Party's nomination in spite of media disapproval and to a considerable degree because of it.

Donald Trump assailed liberal views; though he was not a conventional or establishment conservative—which was worse (since the media knew how to deal with Washington's conservative insiders). Anyway the liberal media heavily favored Hillary Clinton.

Trump was a populist and used social media, especially his twitter account, to make newscasts that the liberal media assumed was its domain. Even more galling, the liberal media had to cover his activities and discuss his agenda thus giving him millions of dollars worth of free publicity.

Also troubling to the liberal media Trump was part of a phenomenon present among many Western democracies: citizens' repudiating big government bureaucracies (labeled the deep state, insiders or the self-anointed political class) that supported certain special interests, political correctness and identity politics.

The liberal media seldom mentioned the "Trump movement" was international in nature. Or that Brexit and the rise of new anti-government political movements and parties came before Trump. The media characterized Trump as the cause not the result—getting the sequence backward.

Donald Trump was candid and blunt, which appealed heartedly to voters that perceived that Washington politicians were not transparent, were out-of-touch establishment figures, were corrupt and did not have the majority of Americans at heart. Trump charged they were destroying America's middle class, the foundation of U.S. democracy.

So the liberal media portrayed Donald Trump as being crude, lacking knowledge about politics, anti-freedom of the press, isolationist, protectionist, racist, misogynist, fascist, a warmonger, and almost everything negative they could think of.

This only got worse after Donald Trump was elected president.

Many of the things the liberal media said and wrote about Trump were mischaracterizations or untruths (or lies). This was considered okay because Donald Trump was their sworn enemy.

The media called the Trump administration secretive, though it had already reported President Barack Obama was one of the most opaque politician ever to sit in the Oval Office. Reporters had also noted that the Obama administration had set a record in ignoring Freedom of Information requests and had used the Espionage Act against whistleblowers who leaked to the press more than all previous administrations combined.

The liberal media made up news about President Trump. Early on the *New York Times* carried a story on Trump badly treating his girlfriends and interviewed one of them. She, Rowanne Brewer Lane, subsequently told *Fox and Friends* that the *Times* had misrepresented her and Trump was kind and thoughtful and was a gentleman.

A host of media outlets (Kellyanne Conway said more than a thousand) carried a news piece about Trump having removed the bust of Martin Luther King from the Oval Office. The reporter that first wrote about this (which others copied without fact checking) admitted he had made a mistake. However, few in the media reported his retraction or that President Obama had removed the bust of Winston Churchill.

The media wrote that President Trump was a protectionist, even though U.S. trade was already out of balance to the degree it was unsustainable and this endangered stable global commerce, and Trump proceeded to fix it.

The liberal media labeled Trump isolationist based on his "make American great again" slogan notwithstanding the fact his rebuilding the U.S. military suggested just the opposite, while he refurbished American alliances and built close personal relations with a host of important world leaders.

Liberals were obsessed to see President Trump fail. They propagated the view of his poor handling of foreign policy on his trip to Asia. However, Asian papers and media outlets said exactly the opposite. Many U.S. news organizations reported China's leader, President Xi Jinping, had bamboozled President Trump even though when in China Trump negotiated the largest economic deal ever for U.S. companies.

The Western media said Trump had surrendered leadership of the world to China; the truth was America's decline was already palpable and was the result of Middle East wars under Bush II and Obama, plus President Obama leading from behind and dramatically cutting U.S. defense spending. Also, never mind that this was a contradiction as the same media fancied downplaying China's expanding global role.

This same U.S. media supported an investigation of the Trump campaign over contacts with Russia that supposedly indicated the latter had influenced the results of the election—even though Russia had intruded into American politics for one hundred years, other nations had certainly influenced U.S, elections and America had tilted elections in other countries for a long time. Plus the evidence indicated the Clintons and the Democratic Party had very questionable ties with Moscow.

The liberal Western media studiously ignored President Trump's accomplishments, such as putting economic growth back on track after eight years of low growth (no GDP rise of more than three percent during any year), a string of stock market records, the lowest unemployment in 17 years, a million new jobs created in six months (pushing Black and Hispanic unemployment to the lowest level ever recorded), the highest consumer confidence for some time, and in general new positive feelings about America.

Patently the mainstream media also underreported other favorable news about President Trump. Considering its salience the defeat of ISIS under Trump was the most slighted event of 2017. Likewise little attention was given to Trump's tax bill and its positive impact on the United States and foreign stock markets and the global economy. And the anti-government protests in Iran, whose leadership President Trump had condemned, got little attention.

The lack of fairness toward President Trump mirrored the fact around 90 percent of liberal media personnel were very pro-Democratic Party and a disproportionate number had supported and/or had given money to Hillary Clinton's campaign. Never was the Western media so slanted in these respects.

Its blatant bias also paralleled, cum caused, a decline in the public's perception of the liberal media's professionalism and its widespread loss of credibility. In fact, Americans' trust in the media dropped below most other institutions and professions.

China has been and is the second mark of the liberal Western media. Why is that?

It starts with the left's view that China is a traditional cum conservative country where liberal ideas espoused by the mainstream media in the United States and Europe are not taking hold and won't. China, it is charged, will not "become like us." China's history and culture are too strong for that, not to mention that Chinese see their country as a past and even current victim of liberal Western countries.

More important, the Western mainstream media dreads China's fast rise, seeing it to be a threat to the liberal world order. In China Western liberal democracy is not an ideology to admire or follow. Rather China is influenced by its history of defining world politics wherein economic influence trumps military power. Already the two financial centers of gravity (the Atlantic and Pacific bloc countries) have been fused into a China-centered one behind Beijing's Belt and Road Initiative and its leading the world in manufacturing, trade and foreign currency, all of which are giving it new global influence.

A secondary impact cum embarrassment of China's global economic dominance is its overtaking Western countries in helping developing countries prosper. Africa is the second fastest growing region in the world for the first time ever; this is because of China's foreign aid and investments. China has been doing more to alleviate global poverty than any other country. Western countries cannot afford to help much any more; developing countries have said this publically to the West's embarrassment.

As a result China is the main driver of planetary growth. According to the World Economic Union, China will account for 35.2 percent of the world's real GDP growth from 2017 to 2019. The United States will provide half of that—17.9 percent. The European Union less than one-quarter of China—7.9 percent. Japan will account for 1.5 percent and Russia 1.0 percent.

So the Western liberal media attacks China, citing a host of its foibles and alleged sins.

It widely and regularly condemns China's "authoritarian dictatorship." Never mind that China's polity historically was a system that operated for the people not of the people or by the people and that it has recently done a yeoman's job of providing for its people—removing 700 million of them from poverty in the last three-plus decades. The government enjoys public acclaim for this.

Forget also the fact that China, which was not historically a country of law, has made tremendous progress in that direction. China has also made big strides in citizen participation in politics. According to Pew Foundation polls its government and leaders have greater citizen support than do the governments in the United States, Europe or Japan. By the way Chinese citizens comment on politics online more than their counterparts in Western countries.

The Western liberal media reports incessantly on the Chinese government's oppressive control of its people, mentioning almost daily its heavy regulation of the Internet and official overreach in controlling crime. They fail to mention, often at least, American and European citizens' growing concern over the deep state at home or that there is widespread blowback against big government intrusiveness in the latter countries.

The liberal Western media frequently cites China for its repression of the population in Tibet. Seldom mentioned is the fact China eradicated Tibet's slave culture (or the fact the Dalai Lama was educated by Nazis) or that protest in Tibet is mostly against local capitalists and not the Chinese government. Because of its misreporting on the Tibet situation and elsewhere, anticnn.com a few years ago became the most popular website for the youth in China.

China is also castigated in the Western media for its terrible air pollution. As a result Westerners have the impression that Chinese cities are the worst in the world in terms of air quality, when the most polluted cities are in the Middle East, India and Africa. Beijing is far down the list at number 57 of 153 in the latest rankings. Considering there are various kinds of air pollution Los Angeles might rank worse than most of China's metropolitan cities.

The liberal media excoriates China for human rights abuses. Ignored is the fact that China's record has improved immeasurable since the passing of Mao and his ultra-leftist, extreme egalitarian regime. Moreover, in terms of race relations, crimes against women, homelessness, the treatment of children and the elderly, public safety and using a number of other measures China does better than the United States.

The Western media blasts China for cheating in its trade relations with other countries even though most countries in the world practice protectionism of some sort. China is singled out because it is bigger economically and for its not being seen as politically correct. Forgotten is the fact that China's trade surpluses increased big-time after it joined the World Trade Organization and that cases filed against China have not proven China to be a big violator of WTO rules. An inconvenient truth is China is such a big competitor in trade mainly because of its higher work ethic, lower taxes and regulations, and fewer lawyers.

The liberal Western media also assails President Xi for having abolished collective leadership in favor of one-man dictatorial rule, ignoring the fact that a meritocracy put him in power; ruthlessness and purges did not. Nor do they mention that more central authority is needed to deal with corruption, lax military discipline, and more hostile enemies on the world stage that abhorred China's rise. The liberal Western media also gives little attention to President Xi's concept of "community of common destiny" as the basis for China's foreign relations though it is praised in non-Western countries.

Meanwhile, Hollywood and academe in the United States, which are in league with the liberal media in their treatment of Chinese, support racial discrimination in admissions to America's top universities (plus liberal professors deliberately give Chinese and other Asians lower grades in their classes than other minorities) while Chinese are by design almost excluded from American movies and television.

In conclusion, it can hardly be said that the Western liberal media bias toward President Trump and toward China is a good thing.

One of the main effects of anti-Trump prejudice is that professional journalism in Western countries, which has long afforded positive and needed connections between the government and its citizens, has been sacrificed. Lost also is its role of protector of fairness and justice.

This is wrong. As Pope Francis recently stated: "Fake news is a sin."

For China, both its citizens and its leaders, Western media bias is seen as part of an effort to contain China, to keep China down, and prevent it from playing a bigger role in international affairs—one that is in keeping with its economic and other advances. Chinese see it as the revival of imperialism, racism and worse.

Many also view Western liberal media bias as likely to bring the United States and China into conflict. In fact, it has been said that the liberal Western media is so obsessed with destroying President Trump and obstructing China's continuing rise that its members think a war between the United States and China might be a good thing. It would be "killing two birds with one stone."

On the other hand, this situation may be one of a "two-edged sword." There is also a positive side to the situation.

In his recently published book *Destined for War*, Graham Allison argues that, learning from the history of the Peloponnesian wars in ancient Greece and most of the major wars since then, the condition of a dominant status quo power and a rising challenging power is the condition that explains wars that followed. Not only that, but the relationship between the United States (the status quo power) and China (the rising power, alas the very fast rising power) now suggests a United States-China war will inevitably result and it will engulf the entire planet.

President Trump and President Xi seem acutely aware of this situation and seek to avoid a conflict. They are also aware of the fact the liberal Western media hate them both and would like to see them in conflict. They thus are making concerted efforts to avoid this.

There is another cause for optimism. United States-China relations have moved from being worse during the later years of the Obama presidency than at any time since President Nixon engineered a rapprochement between the two countries, to the two leaders being cordial and communicating effectively.

Could it be that the intolerance and the hatred espoused by the liberal Western media toward Donald Trump and China might turn out to be a good thing? That would be a huge irony.

SEVENTEEN

Avoiding a United States-China Trade War

Understanding Donald Trump May Help

Just after mid-night on a Friday in June 2018, President Trump announced applying tariffs amounting to $34 billion on certain Chinese goods imported by the United States. The list included water boilers, x-ray machine components, airplane tires and various other industrial parts. China responded tit for tat with tariffs on U.S. products of an equal value: soybeans, pork and electric vehicles.

Although the list did not seem very consequential the liberal Western media responded as if the sky were going to fall. The *New York Times* reported, "Trump's trade war with China is officially underway." CNN reported that the United States (meaning, of course, President Trump) had started the "biggest trade war in history." The *Financial Times* wrote of a coming "three trillion trade war." Associated Press predicted weaker investments, depressed spending, unsettled financial markets and slow global growth, even suggesting Chick-fil-A would lose business because the cookers they use, which are made in China, would now cost more. Some other media outlets predicted the Christmas season that usually boosts the economy would be affected adversely.

For the mainstream liberal media that hate President Trump the expectation (and hope) was that the public fear generated would hurt the president.

What happened? Little or nothing! The U.S. stock market rose; all three of the major indexes (NASDAQ, NYSE, DOW) went up. The Dow jumped by more than one hundred points. Gold and silver (a haven during times of uncertainty) went down. Forecasts for the U.S. economy remained positive. The big stock markets in Asia also rose.

In other words the more cool minds and those that mattered disregarded the Chicken Little hype about a trade war.

The anti-Trump media then shifted gears: if what he just did failed to start a trade war one will certainly happen owing to his future acts. Bloomberg cited former deputy U.S. trade representative under President Obama, Robert Halleyman, who forecast that the present situation would "accelerate like a snow ball going down a hill." *The Atlantic* magazine wrote of Trump already starting four trade wars, with more to follow.

To understand the predicted crisis that did not happen and what might come, one should try to grasp President Trump's thinking on the matter and then decide whether or not bad things forecasted are yet to occur and Armageddon is just over the horizon, or not.

Here are Trump's essential points:

Number one: President Trump believes that free trade is merely an ideal, perhaps just a dream; it is not something that most nations actually practice. The reason is simple. Trade imbalances according to free trade theory (penned by British economist David Ricardo centuries ago) are to be managed by an adjustment of national currencies; countries that have deficits will (or rather should) see an automatic downward movement of their currency and this corrects the imbalance by making their exports cheaper. Unfortunately most nations want to keep their currencies valued low to prevent unemployment and their governments peg them accordingly. They also have a host of other means to keep their exports up and their imports down, such as subsidies, government supports, interest rates controls, and more. Thus the system is plagued by manipulation and does not work to make trade free, or fair.

In the past, Trump notes, American leaders assumed that free trade is something to be adhered to sincerely (while others did not) and the United States was a big loser in trade. Other countries took advantage of America by blocking U.S. imports with more obstacles against U.S. imports than the United States used. A U.S. trade deficit followed—big time. U.S. companies suffered; many collapsed. This situation still obtained when Donald Trump was elected.

President Trump perceives that he must "rock the boat" to change this practice and get a better deal for America. He speaks of a level playing field, fair trade, and reciprocal trade, but he assumes there will be strong resistance to any of these.

Number two: President Trump said the United States might withdraw from the World Trade Organization. To his opponents what could be more heretical?

But maybe Trump is onto something. After China joined the World Trade Organization in 2001 the U.S. trade deficit with China grew much worse. Some even say the WTO caused this. Indeed the WTO helped

China's leaders promote trade, which they did with great verve. China soon became the largest exporting nation in the world. The organization that is responsible for managing world trade and promoting stability therein has plainly not served to balance trade and that is what is awry.

Specifically, the WTO did not and cannot fix (at least in Donald Trump's mind) the U.S. deficit. Indeed it is not equipped to deal with the main causes for it. A nation's (China's in this case) internal commercial practices are at issue. Certainly the WTO cannot command Chinese citizens not to save so much (which allows China lower interest rates and helps economic growth and easier exports) or tell them they should lower their work ethic. It cannot suggest to the United States that its bloated government, with its high taxes and regulations and an expensive welfare and penal systems, are the causes of the trade deficit.

When China joined the WTO President Clinton predicted that it created a win-win situation for the United States and that thousands of new jobs would be created in America. He was very mistaken. Then the situation got worse. Obviously the WTO needs to be revamped or replaced.

President Trump's comment then may be the spark that results in needed reform of the WTO.

Number three: President Trump perceives that the U.S. trade deficit leads to an increase in the U.S. national debt, that is already perilously high (at 21-plus trillion dollars), and threatens the United States and the world financial systems.

Clearly, though some economists disagree, the trade deficit can be connected to America losing many of its industries, higher unemployment (jobs declined by 3.4 million between 2001 and 2015), the need for more government welfare, and larger budget deficits. Few can deny that.

The interest on the U.S. national debt will soon crowd out other items in the budget. It will be larger than defense spending in a few years. More money will have to be raised through taxes and that will make U.S. exports even less competitive.

Patently the situation is unsustainable. Large debt has ruined countries in the past. At some point it will undermine America's global financial leadership—probably sooner rather than later. While China may supplant America's role in managing global trade and more, now it is definitely too soon for that to happen.

The Chinese Yuan still makes up but a quite small portion of global transactions. Anyway President Trump perceives the deficit and the resultant debt are not good for the United States or Americans and something needs to be done. Arguably President Xi and other Chinese officials can identify with President Trump's thinking…and his strategy.

How so? Chinese leaders despise the Western media's fake news that is as anti-China as it is anti-Trump. They have to contend daily with negative press about China from it getting rid of term limits to air pollution and other environmental problems. But more important China's leaders, according to the U.S. media's narrative, want to put an end to the Western liberal world order that Chinese leaders see as based on zero-sum military power theory. That is true. But it is the same antiquated system President Trump attacks and thinks should be reformed or scrapped.

They also understand President Trump's modus operandi: threaten the status quo (and even create chaos and panic) in order to negotiate more successfully. After all this is an essential idea cum strategy in China's diplomatic playbook going back to Sun Tzu, who once said: "In the midst of chaos, there is opportunity."

Thus one might conclude that President Xi is not hyperventilating as the Western media think he is over President Trump's provocations, though he perceives some strong talk in response is normal and proper and is part of the game. President Trump no doubt is able to handle this. In fact, he may welcome it; it adds to the poignancy (and impact) of his declarations.

Thus we need to look at the trade dispute from a different angle. Doing so we should not expect a trade war.

EIGHTEEN

Will the Western Media Prod America and China into a War?

Toward the close of the nineteenth century William Randolph Hearst, who owned the *New York Journal,* and Joseph Pulitzer, who ran the *New York World,* engaged in a spitting contest of sensationalism often mixed with falsehoods to improve the sagging sales of their newspapers.

Then, almost like a gift from heaven for the two, a crisis in Cuba provided them a spotlight. Playing on Spanish Colonial officials' human rights abuses, their untoward acts toward women, their insults aimed at the United States and its citizens, and any incident at the time, the two media moguls, joined by other newspapers, enflamed public opinion in America against Spain.

By most accounts the Spanish-American War of 1898 would not have occurred had it not been for the U.S. media, or at least a good portion of it, especially Hearst and Pulitzer's papers, wanting it and promoting it.

Fast forward to the present.

The Western media currently loathe Donald Trump to a degree almost as intense as Hearst and Pulitzer's aversion toward the Spanish colonial government in Cuba. They are on a tear to do Trump in.

Hollywood and academe in the United States have joined the media's crusade. They too despise Trump with an extreme passion.

During the campaign the three cited Trump for almost every transgression or bad trait they could imagine: his treatment of women, his business practices (including not paying taxes), his espousing protectionism and isolationism, his populism and nationalism, his authoritarian mindset, his racism, and more. Trump was almost *pro forma* accused of lying.

After the election the media kept up its shrill and slanted attacks on Trump. In fact, it got much worse. Newspapers and T.V. reported widely on anti-Trump protest demonstrations giving the impression the majority of Americans detested Trump. Hollywood celebrities castigated Trump in public and won media attention and praise for doing so.

Liberal news establishments reported President Trump suffered from sleep deprivation. They wrote about Trump's mental instability. Both, they said, handicapped his diplomacy. Opinion leaders proffered the view Trump would start a trade war, that his protectionism and isolationism would evoke a global recession, and that he longed to use nuclear weapons. His populism and his authoritarianism, they reported, would spell the end of democracy in the United States and, if Trumpism spread, the rest of the world.

Newspaper and television reporting exaggerated the import of Trump's friendship with Russia and published illegal leaks about Trump's meetings with foreign leaders. The media even reported the U.S. intelligence community withheld information from President Trump saying he could not be trusted.

In any event, what the media said and wrote hinted of discord and even a state of revolt inside the U.S. government. This seriously undermined President Trump's ability to manage foreign policy inasmuch as foreign leaders believed much of what the U.S. media said and thus questioned America's commitments and its ability to act in the event of a crisis.

There was another factor: the U.S. media and their partners had a second enemy. That was China . . .

They had long espoused deep animas toward China. In some ways it was more serious than their ill feelings toward Trump. It had been around longer.

The U.S. media, Hollywood and America's academic community were vexed about the rise of China and the consequences of China becoming a great power and eventually the world's dominant power.

That China had risen was obvious. China had become *the* world's builder. It was the leading dispenser of foreign aid and foreign investments. It was encroaching on America's role in managing the world economy. The "Beijing consensus" had already to a large extent supplanted the "Washington consensus."

Now China is poised to become the world's foremost military power. Its political system is increasingly a model for developing nations and even some developed ones.

These trends indicated the United States would lose its importance and its influence worldwide. With it, liberal values would fade. Asian, cum Chinese values and culture, would replace Western culture.

That would spell the end of the Western dominance of world affairs. It would mean the termination of the Western, liberal world order. This was serious and mightily troubling.

So the Western media and its partners in the entertainment industry and academe decided to "deal" with the "China threat." They had a method: disparage and demonize China.

The U.S. media and academe assailed China's economic system, which they called "market Leninism" (though it was in reality simply a more pure form of capitalism than was being practiced in the West). They assailed China for vast human rights abuses (even though China's rights record had improved markedly since the Mao era and the human condition in China had improved faster than any country in the world due to its highly successful economic growth).

The U.S. media, Hollywood and academe hit China hard for its authoritarian system of governance. China allegedly made little or no progress toward becoming a democracy, though Chinese scholars, and some American pundits, saw China has having an "evaluation democracy" or meritocracy as opposed to America's "election democracy."

Their depiction of China got worse. That China is corrupt was part of the media account of China (though observers had to wonder, since corruption was said to be a drag on economic development, how China could be doing so well while the West was not). China, the media charged, was the champion of launching cyber attacks on the United States (though there was no clear proof offered to substantiate China's guilt other than its growing capabilities in high tech).

China's governance of Tibet, they charged, was oppressive and vile (even though Tibet had experienced unprecedented economic growth, Beijing mostly obliterated what was a kind of slave social system, and violence in Tibet was largely Tibetans against Tibetans owing to jealousy resulting from some succeeding under capitalism and some not). The air in Chinese cities was the worst in the world, they said, though a number of cities in India and the Middle East were much worse.

The U.S. media also propagated the belief that China's political/economic system, and the country itself, were facing imminent collapse. According to the media's narrative China's leaders faced intractable problems, such as debt (though this was mainly internal), while the ruling party depended for its credibility on fast economic growth, and more. The Communist Party, it was said, could not cope.

But the negative news and the predictions of China's collapse were "old hat." As time passed these accounts were discredited. So the Western media had to reset.

One tack was to push China and Trump's America into a conflict. This seemed a good idea since it would amount to killing two (enemy) birds with one stone.

So Western media pundits hyped China's "aggression" in the South China Sea and Trump's threatening China over its presence there. They predicted a naval conflict, one that might well escalate into a broader war.

When China launched its first aircraft carrier, the *Liaoning*, the Western media depicted this as a game changer. The United States, they reckoned, would have to respond in kind.

They advanced the idea that Trump's protectionism and isolationism would mean abandoning the leadership of the world to China. On the other hand (a contradiction) Trump was expected to act to block China's continued rise. His rehabilitating the U.S. military was evidence of this. A conflict would naturally result.

Did the Western media relish a serious escalation of United States-China tensions? It appeared so…

Clearly it would help newspaper circulation. It might also improve the media's image, which was at a historic low.

Would a media promoted war result as it did a hundred and twenty years ago?

"History doesn't repeat itself," Mark Twain once said, "but it does rhyme." The U.S. mainstream media's attacks on President Trump and on China, now frequently in tandem, seem to rhyme enough to be worrisome and even dangerous.

NINETEEN

Understanding the United States-China Impasse on North Korea

The Western press frequently reports the United States and China are at loggerheads in resolving the North Korean threat problem. President Trump has accused China of breaking the UN sanctions by shipping oil to North Korea. China denies the charge.

Some U.S. officials aver China does not really want to help resolve the North Korea menace. The liberal Western media says this.

One might ask: What is going on? Does China want to cooperate with the United States to deal with North Korea, or not?

One way to answer this question would be to look at the problem from China's point of view. Most Western pundits do not do this. The Western liberal media is hostile toward China and eschews talking about China's views and aims.

What are China's interests regarding the North Korea problem?

Plainly China does not favor nuclear proliferation. More nuclear powers to China's leaders means a less stable international system. Global stability is an asset to China, which uses trade to enhance its economic growth and enlarge its global influence that is based on its economic clout.

North Korea's nuclear weapons program is even more a threat to China than to the United States since it is so much closer. Proximity means China is much more in danger.

This reality has recently been underscored by news that one of North Korea's test sites is on the North Korean-Chinese border where earthquakes are possible. This means that a nuclear accident is worrisome. It would gravely affect China's Jilin Province possibly resulting in serious loss of life and injuries to citizens in China.

China regards North Korea as being governed by an outlaw regime. Being seen as China's friend hurts China's global image, which Chinese leaders are promoting with great energy. Chinese leaders hardly want to be associated with a nation whose leader killed his uncle (in brutal fashion) and his half-brother (while he was in another country).

North Korea does not accept China's counsel to restructure its economy, to stop is policies of extorting money by engaging in terrorist activities, to cease its involvement in the illicit drug trade and counterfeiting other countries' (including the United States) currencies.

Bringing this closer to home North Korea has engaged in kidnapping Chinese citizens for ransom while intimidating Chinese tourists.

Plainly China and the United States are generally on the same page regarding how to view the North Korean regime and concur that something needs to be done about North Korea's nuclear weapons and missiles.

Does China have the capacity to influence North Korea? Obviously it does since it is propping up the regime with economic aid and investments, plus trade and more.

There is a "but" here though: North Korea is tough and it has proven time and again it can and will resist China's influence. It addition, it can play China off against Russia and South Korea.

What does China want?

Chinese leaders want to see an end to North Korea's nuclear weapons program and its missile tests. It wants North Korea to cease its bad behavior.

Beijing also wants good relations with the United States, which a resolution to the North Korean peril would facilitate.

What does China not want?

China does not want the North Korean government to collapse. This would mean a million or so refugees might flee into China. This would cause serious problems. Would it use its military to stop this? Machine guns obviously could. But the Western anti-China media would certainly magnify the event and hurt China's global image.

China does not want Korea's unification, which serious actions it takes may precipitate. A unified Korea would mean that U.S. troops in South Korea might move up to the Yalu River that marks the border with China. The last time this happened the result was very bad—the entrance of the Chinese military into the Korean War and that ended in huge causalities for the United States and China.

Sanctions, which if applied too hard too fast, may produce many of the effects China fears. Thus it wants gradual and measured sanctions.

What does China hope for?

Beijing hopes that President Kim will realize his current position is untenable and that changes in policies will be to his advantage and may be his only option; that his survival depends on it. (Kim has thirty of so places where he sleeps because of his worry of an assignation attempt or a U.S, surgical strike; so he must live in constant fear for his life.)

Does China have a "plan B?"

China might be able to instigate an Army coup or something similar (assignation?) to remove Kim from power. China has considerable influence with the North Korean military and its relationship with a post-Kim regime could well be a cordial and workable one. Chinese influence, at that point, might bring about changes China (and the United States) would like in order to resolve the North Korean problem satisfactory to both.

But that is risky. China no doubt prefers Kim remains in power and pursues new "reform" policies.

Another option for China is an oil embargo. But Chinese leaders no doubt see this as extreme and likely destabilizing while thinking it may bring the Army and President Kim closer together. That action would hit the military especially hard.

Chinese leaders have good reason not to trust the United States to keep its present hard policies vis-à-vis North Korea. After all, Washington pursued weak polices and made concessions that bordered on appeasement for more than two and a half decades. Beijing certainly looks at history to guide its decisions, even if they trust President Trump.

Beijing also has cause to wonder (perhaps even doubt) whether President Trump will remain in office. The Western media is almost daily finding fault with him. The U.S. media and the Democratic Party talk of impeachment with regularity. The Mueller team is conducting an investigating of Trump administration's cheating to get elected.

Secretary of State Rex Tillerson declared that the United States does not seek regime change in North Korea and does not intend to pursue Korea unification. But should China believe this? There have been serious rumors in Washington to the effect that Tillerson is unhappy with his position and his relationship with President Trump and that he will leave his job soon. The names of possible replacements have been seen in the media.

Pundits and even former and current officials in the United States frequently offer the opinion that sanctions usually do not work. Indeed the record shows that. Also, the Trump administration does not have confidence in the United Nations and relations with the world body are not good.

Further, the Trump administration's approach is to threaten to use military force if the sanctions do not work.

The best choice is for the United States and China to continue the sanctions and perhaps strengthening them while using diplomatic and economic incentives to get North Korea to change its policies and get rid of nuclear weapons and missiles. Both patience and resolve are needed.

TWENTY

Will President Trump Ignite a War with China?

In recent months much has been said and also written about the United States and China heading toward war. Some say conflict between the two is likely and will be serious. Others say it may be a self-fulfilling prophecy.

Valid or not this is largely a response to trends, but rarified by the brash language and aggressive tone of the U.S. president, Donald J. Trump, and the liberal Western media putting an ominous spin on what President Trump says.

Some of it also comes from President Trump's foreign policy statements and actions that, among other things, provoke China, plus the undeniable fact that China is no longer following the dictum of its former leader Deng Xiaoping that it should be humble and bide its time.

One of the arguments for a coming war is the Thucydides Trap theory advanced in the book by the ancient Greek thinker Thucydides, *The Peloponnesian War*. The argument goes that the situation of a status quo power (in this case Sparta in ancient Greece) and a fast rising power that challenges the former (Athens) creates a condition wherein neither can tolerate the other.

That indeed happened and wars resulted. It occurred many more times in history since. A study of the cases of it happening indicates that now the probability for war is high.

As Graham Allison, director of the Harvard School's Belfer Center for Science and International Affairs, in his new book *Destined for War: Can America and China Escape Thucydides's Trap?* argues the current U.S. relationship with China fits the bill. In fact, the United States is very much a status quo power and China is a fast, very fast indeed, rising power that challenges America.

Another argument is that the decline and possible demise of Western liberalism has created a situation of a pending international system failure cum collapse and collective hostility in the West toward China for causing this. Richard Haass in his book *A World in Disarray: American Foreign Policy and the Crisis of the Old Order and* Edward Luce in his just published book *The Retreat of Western Liberalism* both give dash to this view.

Richard Haass, president of the Council on Foreign Relations, said to be the conscience of officials running U.S. foreign policy, wrote that the Western "liberal democratic global system" whose ingredients are free trade, almost universal economic and social development, progress in human rights, a central role for the United Nations and other international institutions, respect for international law, and nuclear non-proliferation, is now dying.

Luce presents a scenario of war between the United States and China in 2020. The sources: President Trump's ultra-nationalist view that America must "start winning again," areas of conflict that cannot be resolved such as Taiwan and the South China Sea, and advisors Peter Navarro convincing Trump that China must be punished for its harmful trade policies and Steven Bannon telling Trump of an inevitable coming "civilizational showdown" between East and West.

Adding to these arguments is realist political philosophy that has long dominated the realm of thinking cum ideology among both international relations scholars and U.S. foreign policy experts. Realists contend that military power is the basis for the international system and that while arms races are not an existential cause of war, uneven ones definitely are.

What could be more uneven than China increasing its spending on defense by double digit figures since 1990 while the United States and its allies cut their military budgets markedly, cashing in on the so-called end of the Cold War dividend? Then President Obama's deep cuts in the military budget, known as sequestration, furthered this trend.

China's military has also benefitted in spades from buying and acquiring military technology by other means to upgrade the level of sophistication of its military's weaponry. In fact, U.S. experts contend China has made progress faster than expected in almost every realm of its military advances.

Finally, the "Taiwan trigger" for a United States-China conflict cum war has taken on new meaning since the opposition (pro-independence) party won a landmark election in January 2016 and proclaimed China would have to "come to terms." China did not and instead launched a campaign to punish Taiwan thus making the Taiwan Strait again one of the world's most volatile flashpoints.

Inevitably, one is reminded that Taiwan was the cause of United States-China confrontations in the 1950s, an almost crisis in the 1960s, and a face-off of the two country's militaries in the mid-1990s during the

Clinton presidency. Also, it is critical that Taiwan is the only non-negotiable issue between Washington and Beijing based on the fact both countries have in place (conflicting) laws about Taiwan's status and its future. Plus a change in Taiwan's sovereignty would irreparably traumatize United States-China relations.

But how valid are these views? Has the election of Donald J. Trump president of the United States certified them? Is President Trump going to be the immediate and necessary cause of a serious deterioration in United States-China relations that will lead to war?

While the Thucydides Trap indeed seems a valid theory of war and has proven itself a good predictor of 11 of the 15 major wars since 1500 (according to Allison), it did not anticipated correctly the peaceful end of the most recent one: the Cold War.

It may be that the "balance of terror" feature of the United States-Soviet relationship invalidated the "Trap." Or, put another way, collaboration between the two superpowers to prevent the suicide of mankind made a war between them both unthinkable and unlikely.

Plainly there is no good reason to think that President Trump and President Xi do not understand the seriousness of nuclear war or that they are opposed to collusion to make the international system work and not fall into a real war condition (though tension or fake war may be okay).

Luce and Haass agree that the demise of the liberal order and the collapse of a world system based on it have been long in coming. Donald Trump did not cause it. Some in the West seem to have come to the realization that it will be replaced by another system without a war. Some may even think that China's world order may not be a bad one; after all it kept the peace in East Asia for a couple of millennia and is a system based more on construction than destruction.

Worth mentioning in this connection President Trump has signed on to China's mega-construction project the One Belt, One Road, or OBOR, designed to connect the world and facilitate the peaceful development of many countries along the way. President Obama opposed the project and tried (in vain as it turned out) to get U.S. allies to eschew participation.

Donald Trump sent a representative to the opening forum of OBOR in May. He and President Xi are both builders. They see the benefits of building as opposed to making war.

The realists are no doubt correct in saying that an uneven growth of military power is dangerous. Donald Trump is a realist and seems to understand this. Moreover, he is acting to fix the problem by restoring America's flagging military might.

President Trump's reinstating American power is notably more prominent in Asia than elsewhere, with the U.S. Navy getting more ships and more responsibility to keep the balance of power between the United

States and China. It is worth taking to heart the fact the U.S. military budget is now going to grow at a faster pace than China's.

Taiwan is indeed a trigger that might ignite a war between the United States and China. It has become more so with the 2016 election of the pro-independence party's presidential candidate and a plurality of its standard bearers winning seats to the legislature. Cross-Strait relations took a nosedive afterwards.

But conditions have not reached a boiling point. The two world powers are not that far apart in defining their military relationship while Taiwan's economy has grown more dependent on China's and its military grown weaker relative to China's. Both trends make Taiwan less likely to start a conflict without knowing for certain the United States has its back (while Washington keeps its policy on rescuing Taiwan ambiguous).

Meanwhile it is obvious residents of Taiwan are enjoying their peace and prosperity. As one of Taiwan's American friends recently pointed out, the advocates of independence in Taiwan are not so committed as they were in the past. They are arguably not willing to sacrifice their positions, assets and lives in a war they would surely lose for legal separation (Taiwan is already de facto independent) from China.

There are some other facts that appear to instruct that President Trump will not start a war with China.

Shortly after the election and during the transition phase to the Trump presidency, and when speculation was rampant that Donald Trump would destroy United States-China relations, Henry Kissinger (who was advising Trump) went to China and talked to President Xi and other Chinese leaders. Kissinger told them Trump was brash, in-your-face and provocative. This was his style and they need to understand this and deal with it. But, Trump, he said, wants a good relationship with China. Chinese leaders, including President Xi, arguably understand.

Reportedly President Xi (who was also known to be direct and at times provocative) said he could cope with Trump and also wants cordial United States-China relations.

Trump also heeds the advice of former Secretary of the Treasury Henry Paulson who put his ideas on paper in his book *Dealing with China: An Insider Unmasks the New Economic Superpower.* Paulson opines that the United States and China must get along, in fact cooperate broadly, to ensure the international financial system works, that nuclear proliferation is controlled, the global environment is protected, terrorism is dealt with and much more. In fact, Paulson asserts that the global order will be dysfunctional or worse without the United States and China working together.

Another factor, which political theorists can appreciate, is a "convergence" in the composition of the leaderships in the United States and China. Business leaders are now playing a larger role in decision-making in both countries and they are on the same page regarding the need to avoid conflict.

The notion President Trump will incite a conflagration with China is debunked by another significant fact: Trump's granddaughter has been studying Chinese and is using it daily to the degree that she is able to entertain Chinese leaders, including President Xi, in Chinese. What could be a bigger compliment to China? No other U.S. leader has shown this kind of respect for Chinese culture.

Finally, President Trump in his writings and in his public speeches and comments has been very critical of America's recent wars and arguably he is determined to avoid them and will.

Hence, President Trump seems more likely to create the conditions for United States-China peace than his predecessors or what many people think.

TWENTY-ONE

China's Rise as an Innovative Country

Most countries in the world, including the United States, have duly recognized China's rise as an economic and military power. Its accomplishments in science and technology are just as meaningful; in fact, they spur its rise in other realms and make its economic and military prowess assured in the future.

As the record shows, in the last few years China has climbed to the pinnacle of nations of the world in creativity and innovation, especially in areas where it matters. In fact, China has leapt ahead in the race to the top to the degree it has now become noticed and admired but also feared.

In two fields this has special salience: artificial intelligence and quantum computers. Breakthroughs in these two subjects are thought to give China a big advantage in terms of its global power and influence that will propel it to superpower status and beyond.

In 2017 China's State Council approved a blueprint to lift China's artificial intelligence (AI) capabilities such that it will be ahead of all competitors. AI, Chinese leaders believe, and many others agree, will be the key to overall progress in science and technology in the future.

Quantum physics is another field. In 2016, China demonstrated its prowess to the world when it successfully tested a quantum computer that gave it the ability to send messages without worrying they might be hacked. This technology allows things to be at two places at the same time and move through space beyond what seems possible, and accords China a rare strategic advantage.

China's advances in these two areas are not just one-off cases. The world witnessed China's preeminence in a number of other realms before this. In 2010 China's Tianhe-1A was pronounced the fastest computer in the world. In 2012 China set the record for a manned submersible craft, descending more than seven thousand meters into the Mariana Trench.

In 2016, China's Baidu bested all others in human facial recognition. That year China also put the world's largest telescope into use.

This is but a short list. China excelled or passed others in a number of other spheres.

All of this appears to be clear evidence China has jumped ahead of itself, or has exceeded its own rate of progress. It is also proof China has performed better than other countries almost across the board in science and technology and this will impact the nature of an evolving new world order in China's favor.

How does one explain China's sudden and quite unpredicted rise in creativity?

One explanation is that China and Chinese have always been innovative. It is in their DNA. According to Joseph Needham, the renowned author of the multi-volume work *Science and Civilization in China,* historically China was the font of half or more of the world's important inventions.

But China lost this edge several centuries ago. Why? John Fairbank, the noted Harvard Sinologist, contends the reason for this was China's ossified political system. Jared Diamond writes that there was little competitive spirit in China and labor was too plentiful and too cheap thereby discouraging labor saving inventions. Others say that examinations for government jobs and entrance examinations to universities were too humanities-oriented and the Chinese language so difficult it crowded out other learning. Still others suggest it was China's isolationism and/or its self-complacency.

At any rate, owing to recent reforms, China has eliminated most or all of these impediments and is once again highly creative and innovative. One might say it has returned to what it once was.

Another account is Deng Xiaoping's reforms made after 1978. Deng terminated Mao's extreme leftist egalitarianism. He replaced central economic planning with a free market. This opened China to trade and foreign investments and pushed China to become a strong competitor in the international economy and beyond.

Deng's policies also ended poverty and created a middle class of educated citizens. China's colleges and universities were set free from too much oversight while the central government and the party transferred power downward to provincial and local governments. This was a policy of decentralizing decision-making writ large.

Deng's models were the United States beginning two-plus centuries ago and Japan early in its modern history and post-World War II. But Deng's thinking was first and foremost pragmatic. He tried new policies and adopted the best ones.

Deng's successors maintained his policies. Under Jiang Zemin and Hu Jintao China became a moderately prosperous country. It had funds to invest, build and innovate. Of special note China's economic boom continued after 2008 when Western countries entered a recession followed by slow growth (Japan having experienced both after 1991).

Third, is Xi Jinping rise to the position of China's top leader and his keen promotion of innovation.

In 2012 and 2013 Xi became respectively head of the Chinese Communist Party (China's ruling party) and president (head of state). At the time China's economy was booming and it seemingly did not face serious internal or external problems. Yet, China encountered some very pressing "issues": corruption, growing wealth disparities, industrial and environmental accidents, health and safety problems and concern about access to certain natural resources.

Most important, though, was the issue of China's economy being squeezed between lower labor cost countries and technologically advantaged modern countries. Exports, upon which its continued economic growth are linked, were under challenge.

In addition, relations were strained with the United States while the Western media had become hostile toward China, seeing its rise as a threat to the Western liberal world order.

President Xi quickly assumed more authority to govern and deal with these concerns. Xi also had to wrestle with the reality that China's policy established by Deng and continued by his successors to be humble and hide China's accomplishments was no longer sustainable.

President Xi thus promoted his "China dream." There were grounds: China had become an economic leviathan, a fully modern country in many ways, and a contender for global influence with the United Stats. Xi's Belt and Road Initiative (BRI) launched in the fall of 2013 that would link more than sixty countries at a projected cost of $4 to $8 trillion (America's biggest project ever was the Marshall Plan to rebuild Europe after World War II at a cost of just over $100 billion) gave China the title of *the* world's builder. China's continued growth in defense spending coupled with weapons acquisitions and new truly state-of-the-art aircraft and ships made China a regional power and a contender for global power.

President Xi promoted his dream and linked it to innovation in his 2014 book *The Governance of China.* He talked about it in public speeches and in formulating new policies. He allocated funds to various innovative projects. It was a central theme in his keynote speech to the 19th Party Congress in October 2017. He called for efforts to turn China into a "country of innovators" and reach "frontier areas of science and technology."

Given Xi's enhanced political power after the party meeting and his high public approval ratings (the highest among thirty important countries according to the Kennedy School's Ash Center for Democratic Governance and Innovation at Harvard University), he not only leads but inspires others as well.

Fourth, China's political system is a meritocracy, which embraces a template that searches, chooses, trains and retains talented personnel. It promotes the best of these to more important jobs with greater responsibilities. This is essential to progress in science and technology. It is critical to creating a culture of innovation.

Chinese leaders are also instilled with nationalistic and patriotic sentiments and espouse views for improving the country so that China's status and influence in the world will steadily improve.

This seeps down. Political surveys in China show that there is backing for China's meritocratic system among China's "best and brightest." A recently done survey at Qinghua University, China's MIT, showed 28 percent of undergrads, 43 percent of graduating seniors and 55 percent of graduate students join the Communist Party.

This builds public confidence. A study published two years ago on trust in government done by the Pew Foundation and based on opinion polls taken in a host of countries concluded that public trust in China was consistently in the 80 percent range; in the United States it was below 40 percent.

Chinese also make comparisons. Officials in most Western democracies have become self-serving, corrupt and out of touch with their citizens. As a consequence a diminishing portion of the population of the United States, European countries and Japan feel that democracy is a good political system.

A fifth reason for China's leap forward in science and technology is its formidable financial power, in other words it has the money to finance research—which is often very expensive. Some say this is the main reason for China's success in science and technology.

This happened because of Deng's economic reforms generated impressive GDP growth. For some years GDP increases were annually double digit (called miracle growth). But a high savings rate and a large favorable balance of trade were also important. Saving rates reached 60 percent—the highest rate ever recorded for a big country. China's global trade became the largest of any country in the world and exports exceeded imports by a large margin.

By the turn of the century China had become a large holder of foreign exchange while household and company assets had also grown exponentially. In 2006, China passed Japan to become the world's foremost holder of gold and foreign currencies—those having increased by six fold since 2001. The next year China's foreign exchange amounted to one and a half trillion U.S. dollars.

Today China's foreign exchange totals over three trillion dollars (not including Hong Kong's four hundred-plus billion). This figure is more than two and a half fold Japan's (that is number two in the world). The United States is not on the list of the top twenty countries.

Because of this China is able to finance large increases in research and development. In fact, Chinese R&D has been growing by seventeen to eighteen percent annually, while the United States, Europe and Japan are increasing their R&D spending by two to three percent a year—close to the rate of inflation.

China can allocate billions of dollars to big scientific and technology projects. It is a matter of record China is easily outspending the United States, Europe or Japan in critical areas. According to Arthur Herman, a senior fellow at the Hudson Institute, the European Union has allocated slightly less than a billion euros over the next ten years to quantum research. The United States is spending $200 million a year. China is investing $10 billion to just one project it will complete in the next two and one half years.

To advance its work in artificial intelligence China has allocated billions of dollars. American scientists have noted that the United States has neither the money nor a plan to compete with China.

A sixth explanation for China's leap in innovation and its technological progress is the fact China was humiliated by the West for a hundred and fifty years since the Opium War. Both China's leaders and the Chinese people are driven to rectify this.

Ironically the liberal Western media amplifies this feeling with its biased reporting on China's rise that it sees as portending the destruction of the Western-built liberal world order. This prompts Chinese to recall more vividly their past victimhood and view the Western media's bias as disdain of China, jealousy and racism. It motivates them to aim higher and do better.

Interestingly, Chinese regard prejudice as not necessarily bad and even a positive thing; they use it to advance nationalism. Specifically they cite it as the basis for China and its citizens' strong desire to excel.

A seventh point is that Chinese are a networking people and government policies of encouraging use of the Internet and other means of communicating makes this a contributing factor in China's boom in innovation. There are more people using the Internet in China than in the United States.

John Naisbitt, the famous futurologist and author of *Megatrends: Ten New Trends Transforming Our Lives* and the book *China's Megatrends: The 8 Pillars of a New Society* argues that networks help Chinese succeed in not only business but in other endeavors as well, including work in science and technology.

Chinese indeed interact easily with other Chinese and with foreigners in their work and in particular in their drive to innovate. This amplifies China's advantage in its sheer numbers of students, its bountiful talent, and massive data collected and codes written. It gives China a special (huge) edge over other countries such as Japan that is highly technology-oriented and does advanced research in many fields but does not network well.

Speaking of networking, China also sends more students abroad than any other country in the world. Most go to the United States where they can learn about creativity. This amplifies their proclivity to interact. They are focused on engineering, mathematics, physics and chemistry to fulfill the old Chinese adage that these fields open them the world.

In conclusion, China is on the cusp of becoming an innovation powerhouse. The world will be a different place, a better place, for it. Of course, there are detractors.

TWENTY-TWO

Why the United States is Losing (has lost?) the Number One World Power Ranking to China

According to recent opinion polls taken in the United States asking the question what country in the world is the most powerful the answer given is China. The *U.S. News and World Report* surveys on this subject are the most telling.

In other words, to Americans the United States has lost its status as the world's preeminent power and China has won that status.

How does one explain this? Residents of other countries do not agree, though they certainly confirm the fact China is a fast rising power and deserves a higher ranking among nations in power and influence status.

The reasons Americans rank China as the strongest country in the world are numerous. Here is a start: President Bill Clinton demeaned the United States morally when he was president. George W. Bush spent trillions of dollars on wars in Iraq and Afghanistan that wasted America's treasure (including thousands of lives and severe injuries to many U.S. soldiers. The wars proved little or nothing. Barack Obama adopted a policy of America "leading from behind" (which meant not leading at all to many) and oversaw the worst recovery from a recession in American history.

A more immediate cause of the polls showing Americans believe China is the world's leading power was the election of Donald J. Trump president. The mainstream liberal news media hate Trump and do everything it can, including disseminating fake news, to portray him in a bad light. One of the favorite narratives is that Trump has caused the United States to surrender (to China) its number one position in the world.

It is said Trump compromised making American great again in signing the 2017 budget agreement, which will add a trillion dollars a year to the U.S. debt that was already a massive $21 trillion. This will lead to the devaluation of the dollar and America's fall. That happened to the U.K. in the mid-1950s when its financial condition did not allow it to pursue an aggressive policy at the time Egypt seized the Suez Canal. After this Britain fell fast in its world power status.

Even if Americans are wrong about China's fast rise, there are a plethora of believable arguments that this will happen in the future, sooner rather than later. In other words, America has little hope of competing with China going forward.

The arguments for this position go further than those just stated.

First, China is larger than the United States in land area. It is more than four fold the United States in population. Simply thinking that if equality prevails in the world, as seems to be happening and as the liberal Western world order dictates, China will become number one.

Second, China has a long history of being the leading country in its world—East Asia. China's diplomacy created the rules for the relations of nations in that part of the world. China was a large and successful empire. It is apparently that again. History is simply repeating itself.

Third, there have been many doubters of China's rise. Some cite the threat Japan posed to the U.S. global leadership up to and during the 1980s. Then Japan fell from grace. China will do the same. But those that said this have been proven terribly wrong. Others mention China's foibles: a one party system, a weak banking system, etc. These things it was thought would spoil China's hopes to continue as as *the* formidable rising power. But China's collapse has not happened. In fact, the failed predictions of China's demise makes it look stronger.

Fourth, China has no peers in challenging America's superpower (sometimes hyper power) status. Europe, Russia and Japan are sometimes cited. But all are patently declining powers facing demographic, economic, and a military loss of status. India is rising, but it is too far behind China to be considered a serious contender. Belief in a coming multipolar world, in which there are five or more powers, has thus faded.

Fifth, is America's assumption cum policy (and that of the West in general) it would able to cope with China's rise was founded on the idea that China's very successful economic development would beget democracy, that China could be induced to become a stakeholder in the liberal world order and that it would accept Western values across the board. These thoughts have all been proven misguided.

Sixth, instead China is propagating its "China Dream," the essence of which is China will be a great power and it will do so on China's terms, not accepting the West's bromides any more. This happened rather suddenly. China's former leader Deng Xiaoping advocated China not proclaim its rise and hide its accomplishments. President Xi Jinping is saying the opposite. There has been blowback in the United States. Part of that is loss of self-confidence that anti-Trump forces encourage. Trump's enemies are convincing and are an obstacle to him fulfilling his dream.

Seventh, Western democracy, that has long been thought to be the bulwark for pushing back against China's rise, is on the skids. This was noticed more than two decades ago when developing countries ceased being enthusiastic about democratization, as it did not facilitate economic growth as it once did. Thus the "Third Wave" of democratization in the world ended. As it did many accepted the "Beijing consensus" in in lieu of the "Washington consensus."

Eighth, recently a decline in support of democracy has been evident in Western countries; their political systems have become dysfunctional and public support for democracy is waning fast. At the root of this problem is the fact that in mass democracies politicians running for office habitually promise more than they can deliver knowing that they can create debt that will not come due before they leave office. Scottish Professor Alexander Taylor wrote that democracies last 200 years and then they crash owing to their natural evolution toward mass democracy of this sort. Many Americans seem aware of this.

Ninth, the Western mainstream media, especially in the United States, espouse hate and bias toward China viewing it as a threat to the Western liberal world order. They thus castigate China for its authoritarian system, it disrespecting human rights, and bullying other countries. They patently downplay the fact China has done more than any country in the world in reducing global poverty (including it being the driver behind fulfilling the UN's Millennial Goals), that China has done more to facilitate economic development among poor countries (to the degree Africa is the second fastest growing region of the world in gross domestic product, which it never before experienced, thanks to China's foreign aid and investments and is appreciated as seen by the fact that 70 percent of Africans have a positive view of China). This makes China look strong and the United States appear weak.

Tenth, liberals in the United States have supported a system of discrimination against Asians, affecting Chinese the most, in admission to America's top colleges and universities. They sanction what amounts to racism. This they justify because they see China as a rising military power as shown by its astounding progress in making new cutting-edge weapons and its big increases in defense budgets (even though most experts say China is at least a decade behind the United States in military strength—with one military base abroad and few allies, while the United States has hundreds).

Eleventh is the fact most Americans realize that capitalism is a superior system to socialism in terms of generating wealth and power, even though there is growing support for the latter in the United States. Forty years ago when the United States was commandingly strong in the world and China was weak America was capitalist and China was socialist cum communist. In 1978 Deng Xiaoping assumed the helm of political power and transformed China it into a free market capitalist country. Meanwhile the United States was fast evolving into socialism with its big government and a growing welfare state. A codicil of this change was a reversal in the trade balance between the two that favored China to the degree that China now accounts for nearly half of America's trade deficit, which has destroyed America's belief in and (apparently?) its practice of free trade. As U.K economist James Goldsmith warned a number of years ago, free trade cannot be sustained between capitalist and socialist counties. What he said is now obvious (with calls for managed trade) while one of America's fundamental truths (free trade is good) is no longer gospel. Yet, free trade, Americans think, must be propounded by big powers.

Twelfth, China has accumulated financial resources as a result of its high proclivity to save and its foreign trade surpluses such that it can engage in building projects of the scope America cannot contemplate. One of them, the Belt and Road Initiative (BRI), will connect China with Central Asia, Europe, the Middle East, Africa, South Asia and Southeast Asia, integrating economies into China's along the way. When finished it will be a $6 to 8 trillion undertaking. America's biggest such project was the Marshall Plan after World War II that facilitated the recovery of Europe at a cost of just over one hundred billion (in current dollars). The BRI has already undermined the bipolar nature of global financial power (the United States/Europe bloc and the East Asia bloc) into one bloc centered in China. It is also turning China's Yuan into a global currency to compete with the dollar, which is fast losing its shine due to America's huge and unsustainable debt.

Thirteenth, China's huge accumulation of money has also made it possible to increase its spending on research and development by 18 to 20 percent annually, while the United States can afford only 3 percent increases. China is now registering more patents than the United States each year. It has become the world's leader in green energy. It leads the world in robotics, and much more. It has 99 percent of the world's electric busses on the road.

Fourteenth, Americans admire and respect China's rich culture, though they are also threatened by it. Americans naturally make comparisons. The United States is suffocating from financial overhead because of expensive government welfare programs, the scourge of illegal drugs, crime and a very costly penal system, children born out of wedlock, and illegal immigrants. Despair and pessimism about America results. Suicides are up markedly in every U.S. state but one. 60 percent of Americans believe their children will not be as well off as they are. China does not have such problems anywhere close to their magnitude in the United States.

Fifteenth, futurists who look for factors that will in particular enhance a nation's global power status cite two: artificial intelligence and quantum computers. The United States is slated to spend hundreds of billions of dollars to advance its capabilities in these two areas. China is allocating trillions.

Many would say that Americans overestimate China's influence in the world because of America's problems. Others might say that they are simply looking ahead. In any case, the trends are clear. Learning from China might help. But that would require a transformation of the kind most politicians say is not what America is.

TWENTY-THREE

Will China Meddle in America's Mid-term Election?

In mid-year 2018 American media savants began speculating that China may attempt to influence the coming U.S. election. Some even said that effort had already begun.

What was the evidence?

Former Chinese tycoon now exiled in the United States, Guo Wengui, said so. He noted that China had just interfered in an election in Cambodia; more he suggested are to follow. At the time an official in Beijing said publically that a Trump election victory in November would "set them back 100 years."

There was more . . . President Trump tweeted that referencing his opposition that "the fools have focused on Russia and should look in another direction, China." John Bolton, Trump's national security advisor, said there is concern about Chinese meddling.

This seems credible prima facie evidence to make the case China wanted to throw the November U.S. election to the Democrats. There was more to say.

China has developed the capabilities to interfere in U.S. politics through the Internet and cyber-warfare. According to Adam Segal (writing in the recent issue of *Foreign Affairs* magazine) the United States has already "ceded leadership in cyberspace to China." Further, he says that China "aims to build an impregnable cyber defense system, giving itself a greater voice in Internet governance...and lead the globe in advanced technologies."

China sending more students to U.S. colleges and universities (especially to study the hard sciences and computers), by far than any other country, and putting an emphasis on computer and cyber related subjects in Chinese universities is additional evidence it wants to dominate the world in these fields in the future and the United States is an obstacle to China attaining that objective.

Not only does China have the capabilities to gather intelligence in (and on) United States, it is doing exactly that. China has managed to filch high tech trade secrets from U.S. companies in large quantities. China (presumably its intelligence agencies) managed to lift, it is said, 20 million classified personnel files on American government employees and the employees of companies contracting with the U.S. government. In recent years China has spent billions of dollars to grow its media influence in the United States.

Another reason for thinking China is planning to influence the coming U.S. election is that President Trump's policy of applying tariffs on Chinese imports (which last year were $500 billion-plus, constituting a huge portion of China's exports) has caused such disruption in China that according to some sources it has led to serious infighting in the government and to a state of "policy paralysis." The Western media has even reported that President Xi's leadership has been affected and that the "China dream" has been undermined.

There is hard data to support this view: China's economic growth and stability have been dented. Manufacturing indexes are down, consumer confidence is sliding, and the stock market has experienced a negative trend. There is even an increase in failed land auctions while local governments are facing funding problems.

Chinese pundits are saying United States-China relations are "more dangerous" than in the past 40 years. Chinese officials allude to the fact they originally assumed Trump was taken in by their adulation and friendly diplomacy and they did not, therefore, need to adhere strictly to their promises of fixing the trade imbalance (which got worse). But that turned into Trump applying even tougher policies, prompting fear of a trade war.

China's leaders adopted hard policies in reaction lest they lose face. China even slapped tariffs on goods coming from critical Trump voting constituencies. But it soon appeared China was losing the contest.

Some even sensed that the trade war might lead to a real war. Trump's National Defense Strategy report labeled China a "strategic competitor." Chinese leaders said America is no longer regarded as China's friend, and they would find it difficult to negotiate with an enemy. This, some say, changed China's perspective on President Trump.

So why not wish Trump's Republican supporters in Congress would lose the 2018 election and act accordingly?

There are counterarguments! In other words there are the reasons to believe China is not interfering in America's coming election and will not?

First, it is an old fundamental principle of China's diplomacy: Do not interfere in the domestic affairs of another country. This has long been

China's mode of conducting foreign policy and has been appreciated by nations China has dealt with. It also justifies China's resistance to others criticizing its style of governance, human rights, and otherwise interfering in China's domestic politics.

Even though China has become a much bigger power in recent years and can, and sometimes needs to, interfere in the internal matters of other countries, it has not made this a practice. In fact, it has kept the tradition of non-interference in other countries' politics. There is no serious reason to think that China will now adopt a different policy.

Anyway, Chinese leaders are very aware of the blowback in America from Russia's efforts to influence a U.S. election. So why risk it? It makes little sense and perhaps no sense at all since China seeks to maintain close relations with the United States to buy U.S. high tech firms and purchase U.S. technology. Trade with the United States is also critical to China.

Another reason for eschewing involvement in a U.S. election and thus being charged with interfering in America's domestic politics is that this would invite retaliation. The United States invented the Internet and still sets its standards. American companies are still on the cutting edge of research in this area.

Moreover, the United States has demonstrated it is very talented at using cyber warfare weapons against another country. In 1999 during NATO bombings in Yugoslavia U.S. covert intelligence operatives made Serbian air defenses believe U.S. planes were coming from the opposite direction they actually were. Later America made the work involved in Iran producing a nuclear weapon go awry (literally explode) and caused a big setback to Iran's nuclear weapons program (recall Stuxnet). This indicates Washington has considerable capabilities to inject its influence into others' internal affairs.

There are some other good reasons to believe China is not makings efforts to influence America's coming election, nor will it.

First, the Western liberal media harbors serious antipathy toward China. Most of all they abhor China's rise because it is destroying the liberal world order. They also dislike China's authoritarian politics and its human rights policies. Thus the narrative that China is or may mess with the U.S. election is spread with no real evidence this is so. Moreover, the case that Russia interfered with the last election has grown old and is not having much impact any more; the media needs a new villain.

Second, it is election season in the United States and politicians and their promoters and advertisers as well as the U.S. media like scapegoats. Since Americans are jealous of and fearful of China it is a prime target. This has been true of past elections. Thus it is natural to vilify China more than usual during election campaign and it is now handy to charge China with election interference.

Chinese leaders are quite aware of these two points.

Third, while China's populace to some degree is distressed with President Trump they still regard him highly. They perceive he resembles their own leader, President Xi, whom they highly respect. They still believe Trump reveres and likes China. Asking Chinese on the street about Donald Trump the common answer is they admire him. The wish that Hillary Clinton had won the election is something that is almost never heard. Chinese leaders as well as the population alike have better feelings for Republicans than Democrats; Republicans have long treated China better. Last but not least most of Chinese leaders are optimistic that relations with President Trump will improve. Most also understand that America's trade deficit with China is not sustainable.

Thus one should not anticipate China will mess with the U.S. election and be skeptical when it is said it is. Certainly no one should take too seriously what a Chinese exile says or the reports from the hate China media in the United States. Also one should ignore the harsh words exchanged between President Trump and Chinese leaders; that is their way of negotiating.

TWENTY-FOUR

Does President Donald Trump Dislike China and Chinese? On the Contrary!

Recently a number of stories have appeared in the Western liberal media pushing the narrative that President Trump despises both China and Chinese people. The former stems from comments he has made in conjunction with the tariffs he has applied on Chinese products entering the United States, the hurt this has caused China and the likelihood of a trade war.

The second is an outgrowth of the idea that Trump is a racist, a view his opponents advanced during the election campaign in 2015-16 and have been propagating ever since.

The two themes, in tandem, are useful to the Democratic Party going into an election in November. While only a legislative election it is a critical one and Donald Trump is the salient issue of the campaign for Democrats.

Are the charges true? The facts speak otherwise.

Donald Trump's life and his experiences doing business with and what he has said about China and Chinese is a good place to start.

During his younger days conducting business in New York City (where there are more Chinese than any other American city) Trump often dealt with China and Chinese. He had business deals with Chinese. He rented property to Chinese. If he didn't like them this would likely not have been true.

Not only that but at the top of his list of recommended books is Sun Tzu's book *The Art of War.* The list also contains four other books about China including Henry Kissinger's book *On China.*

A few years ago Trump encouraged his grandchildren, with whom he is close, to study Chinese and speak it daily. They did, and do, that; they have even conversed with and entertained top officials from China, including President Xi and his wife, the First Lady, in Chinese. Few other Americans, much less its top leaders, can say that.

President Trump has also praised the Chinese people and Chinese culture in his public discourse. He has related very well with Chinese leaders that visited the United States and when he visited China.

In his book *The Art of the Deal,* Trump made an issue of the huge trade deficit the United States had with China and the corrosive affects this had on America. But he did not blame China for this; he castigated American leaders for allowing it to happen and all that came with it: the loss of American's jobs, the shuttering of American companies, and an unbearable U.S. debt.

Unlike the liberal Western press, which fears and hates China for it being an existential threat to the liberal world order and pictures it as a destroyer of the Western world by supplanting it with its own "China Dream," Donald Trump is not part of that crowd.

The Western media likewise is full of condemnations of China for its authoritarian system, citing President Xi for getting rid of term limits (though Chinese citizens and the media in developing countries have not expressed alarm) and human rights abuses (even though China's human rights record is infinitely better than it was in the past and many world leaders agree with China's view, as formalized in the Bangkok Declaration, that states that in assessing a nation's human rights conditions one needs to consider its history and culture. Also China does not have some of the serious problems seen in the United States and other Western countries, such as crime, the status of elders, etc.

The Western liberal press is now regularly criticizing China's Belt and Road Initiative (BRI) that will link up much of the world in trade and other commerce and will be a boon to developing countries. Donald Trump did not join that chorus. In fact, he praised the BRI and even led American companies to participate. He also promised, and so acted, to terminate the Trans-Pacific Partnership agreement, a plan to regulate trade engineered by the Obama administration that was patently anti-China and specifically targeted China's economic influence globally.

President Trump has instead lauded China's economic progress and its role in getting rid of world poverty and helping developing nations. The liberal Western media ignore these accomplishments.

Regarding Chinese in America, their number one complaint is the discrimination their children encounter in applying for admission to top U.S. colleges and universities. When polled Chinese Americans say Boston is the worst U.S. city in terms of bias toward Chinese—because of the many top universities there that have policies to exclude or limit the number of Chinese students.

Recently a group called Students for Fair Admission on behalf of Asian Americans sued Harvard University for racial discrimination over its admissions policies. The organization complained of the university using quotas and "likability" and "kindness" as criteria to weed out Asians (who are by culture more quiet and unassuming).

Among Asians that have complained and that have backed the suit against Harvard's Chinese students have been the most numerous and the most committed.

The Trump administration just recently gave its support to the Asian students in their lawsuit against Harvard. The administration's position is that admissions should be without racial discrimination to be "conducted lawfully." Some Trump officials expect the case may go to the Supreme Court where conservative judges will support the students as opposed to liberal judges that like affirmative action.

Still another way of ascertaining whether Trump dislikes Chinese as the liberal media contends is the case is to ask the Chinese for their views.

As is widely known Chinese see events and issues from a historical perspective more than others. How then do they see history as it relates to this question?

For a large proportion of Chinese their modern history begins with the Opium War, which to them marks a century-plus of humiliation that they are recently leaving behind as a product of Deng Xiaoping's free-market reforms that have produced astonishing economic growth and have made China a major world power.

When they think and speak of the Opium War, they also remember the name Warren Delano—an American businessman cum smuggler who took over the opium trade when the Chinese shut out the British from the business. Delano made millions.

Warren Delano was President Franklin Roosevelt's grandfather and the source of his middle name and his considerable wealth.

FDR was also an enthusiastic supporter of Chiang Kai-shek and helped him execute a devastating civil war in China after World War II against Mao and his followers. FDR was, of course, a Democrat and a liberal icon.

Meanwhile, at the end of World War I, President Woodrow Wilson, another Democrat and arguably the most racist among U.S. presidents, sold out China at the peace talks in Versailles. Wilson caved in to Japan's predatory demands on Chinese territory even though China was on the victor's side during the war. China's diplomats walked out of the talks and remained forever bitter about Wilson's "betrayal." Chinese remember this vividly.

Chinese also recall that it was President Harry Truman who launched a war against China during the Korean conflict, resulting in 180,000 Chinese killed (according to a recent Chinese accounting not previously stated with precision)—half of the total number of soldiers that died in Korea. Mao's son was among them.

They remember that President Nixon, a Republican, made peace with China when Democrat presidents Kennedy and Johnson would not. Nixon put U.S. relations with China on a new and friendly basis that according to Chinese (and other) historians changed the course of history.

Finally, in spite of the recent tiff over tariffs Chinese leaders speak highly of President Trump. According to Michael Pillsbury author of recently published *The Hundred-Year Marathon* and arguably the top American China scholar in terms of dealing with and understanding China's leaders, Trump is seen as highly intelligent, an able negotiator and someone China can be friends with.

The same goes for the man on the street in China. Recent pollsters have concluded Trump is both admired and liked by the Chinese people. One recently reported he met no one that wished Hillary had been elected.

Like Chinese in China American Chinese and recent Chinese immigrants in the U.S. talk about President Trump on their websites. They describe him as decisive, strong, businesslike, and straightforward. They like his hard line on crime and even his immigration policies as they apply to illegals, whom they say create a danger to them and "break the queue" to get government benefits that few Chinese enjoy and instead pay for. They say Chinese are not like other immigrants that come to America for welfare, other handouts and an easy life. Surveys show the longer Chinese are in the United States and the more education they have the more they support Trump.

The inescapable truth is President Trump is too much a pragmatist to be racist. He despises identity politics and says he wants to make American great again. This may be defined as nationalism but it has reduced unemployment and despair and has improved the lot of almost all Americans but especially minorities.

Trump is also a businessman with the ability to recognize talent. He knows full well that Chinese have contributed greatly to progress in science and technology and much more in the United States. He has said so frequently.

Democrats that charge Donald Trump with hating China and Chinese are employing an old strategy of accusing their opposition of misdeeds and nefarious views that are their own in order to divert attention from the latter.

TWENTY-FIVE

Dealing with the U.S. Trade Deficit with China

In recent weeks the U.S. trade deficit with China and President Trump's efforts to fix it have been considered so serious many pundits say that it imperils economic relations between the two major global economic powers and the contagion will spread around the world. Former Federal Reserve Chairman Alan Greenspan recently warned that the United States is "on the brink of a trade war."

The magnitude of the deficit confirms this narrative. In 2017, America's trade deficit totaled a whopping $566 billion—the world's largest. America's trade deficit with China was $375 billion. This shortfall eclipsed the U.S. deficit with any other country: $71 billion with Mexico $69 billion with Japan, $65 billion with Germany. In fact, it almost equaled the red ink in the trade ledger with all other nations combined.

The situation has recently gotten worse. It is obviously unsustainable.

The consequences of the deficit explain the gravity of the situation.

America has lost many of its industries. Manufacturing jobs declined by 34 percent from 1998 to 2010 and continued to disappear after that. In response the government expanded payments to the needy including unemployment benefit (that turned into long-term disability for many during the Obama years). The welfare state increased in size and permanence. The U.S. debt grew exponentially and became unsustainable.

As a result there are two inconvenient and painful truths: One is the United States and China have changed the natures of their economies. America was once (when it had a trade surplus with China before 1980) a capitalist country; China was a socialist country. Now they are reversed. Since socialism cannot compete with capitalism China has been winning in trade competition. Two, the U.S. trade deficit has resulted in America accumulating a huge debt—recently totaling more than 21 trillion dollars.

This undermines the role of the United States overseeing the global financial system.

The U.S. budget line item for interest on the national debt crowded out other items. The government's help to business declined and so did exports. Countries, i.e. China, with budget surpluses faced the opposite situation. China could afford more money to help its exporters and for R&D to bolster its promising industries and companies.

A secondary effect was that China invested much of the funds gained from its trade surplus with the United States in America and the U.S. debt to China grew, to $1.17 trillion as of January 2018, or 19 percent of the public U.S. debt owned by foreigners. If China were to cash in much of this it would cause interest rates in the United States to spike and jolt the housing market. That might set off a U.S. recession that would become global.

China has also been using its trade gains to buy U.S. companies and invest in others. This constitutes another problem. It is already an election issue.

Free trade is supposed to resolve this problem. But it is an ideal; in reality it is little more a cliché than a policy that is truly practiced. Ideally currency devaluations would resolve a trade imbalance. But using this mechanism causes others to employ it too in order to remain competitive; it thus invites currency wars. Anyway the U.S. dollar is a global tender and must remain stable and strong for the global financial system to function properly. A strong currency is also necessary if the United States is to remain a global superpower, as it so desires.

Hence the global financial system is not working. Yet the politicians still speak of free trade as if it is desirable and will fix all problems.

Who is to blame for this situation? Those quick to judge say it is China cheating in trade. This is the bromide of the Western mainstream media that despises China because it is destroying the liberal world order and supplanting it with its own. Anyway politicians love scapegoats.

So, China is said to be protectionist. According to the narrative, it undervalues its currency (so that it can sell more goods) and steals intellectual property from foreign enterprises (so it can move up the innovation curve quickly and at little expense).

But are these charges true? If they are, are they meaningful?

China is, of course, protectionist. But so are most nations. China's protectionism is not worse. In fact, China's trade surplus increased after it joined the World Trade Organization that is the overseer of global trade. China's protectionism cum mercantilism is more destabilizing almost solely because China's economy is so large. It is reasonable China be judged by how big its economy is? Not if rules are to work.

China's currency, it is said, is undervalued. But some say it is overvalued. If China wants to be a bigger player in global finance as its critics say, and fear, its currency should be overvalued. But the Chinaphobes don't want China's dominance in international economic affairs! Anyway a number of top economists argue its currency valuation is not an important factor in explaining the U.S. trade deficit with China.

Is China pinching intellectual property? The answer is yes; but there is more to say than that. Most nations do this. Again it is a matter of China's size. Also China is more successful at it than most because it presents it as a bargain—technology for access to the huge and growing China market. U.S. companies are not forced to give up their technology.

In any case, China is putting more money and resources into advancing its technology (around 18 percent annual increases in R&D spending compared to the United States 3 percent). As a result it is registering more patents each year and is making more technological breakthroughs than the United States. Hence American companies are now eyeing China's technology and it will not be too long before the technology-taking situation is reversed.

Given the charges against China are not wholly convincing, one might conjecture that the problem lies with what the United States is not doing right. The obvious best solution to the problem is for the United States to export more to China. (Blocking imports from China will be badly inflationary and patently runs the danger of engendering a trade war.)

Two obstacles that are of the upmost importance in making it possible for the United States to export more to China are high taxes (U.S. corporate taxes have been among the highest in the world) and burdensome regulations that many business leaders say are a worse hindrance.

President Trump has taken meaningful actions to rectify both. And his efforts have had a major impact. GDP growth, investments, and employment are all up. But the advantage is still with China. Can he do more? Doubtful; the politicians stand in his way.

In looking for other solutions Trump and his advisors need to consider the United States needs to reduce its huge and smothering debt. In 2017 the federal government took in $3.3 trillion in taxes. Yet spending exceeded that by $665 billion. The cause is members of Congress pander for votes by offering government goodies. That is the way America's mass democracy works these days: politicians promise benefits to the poor for votes knowing they will be out of office before the bills comes due.

Even President Trump's recent budget is full of this kind of spending. Trump had to compromise to get other things he wanted, including more money for defense, and the debt grew even bigger.

The two biggest government outlays are health care and social security. Health care costs in the United States are almost the highest in the world and are expected to increase by 6 percent annually for at least a decade. Social security expenditures will grow as a result of aging and more people retiring. Will either be fixed, or will the politicians simply kick the can down the road? There is little optimism around.

The federal government's budget also includes a line item for interest payments amounting to 7 percent of total spending. Some projections are that this will more than double in five years at which time the amount needed for interest payments will exceed spending on national defense.

Meanwhile interest payments will affect everything else in the budget. Especially important in terms of the question at hand it takes away money for improving America's dilapidated infrastructure and reduces spending on R&D, upon which product advances depend (i.e. keeping up with the innovation curve).

Looking ahead, in less than a decade entitlements and the interests on the debt together will consume one hundred percent of taxes paid. Still politicians don't offer any meaningful answers. The political left wants more taxes to pay for these things but don't think of the consequences.

There are also many costs outside the budget and they are a big drag on business, and exports. Again the solutions to trammeling these expenditures are political and nothing curative is in sight.

The cost of lawyers in the United States is an enormous burden on doing business. Liability costs as a percentage of the gross domestic product are two and one half times the average of countries in the Eurozone. They are many fold China's.

Little to nothing is being done to change this. It is no wonder many say the United States is a nation of lawyers and note that expertise in law unfortunately is the main, cum "required," background of members of Congress. This is seldom the training of high officials in China. Meeting growing legal requirements not only are costly to the United States but also results in long delays in getting things done.

Not unrelated to this problem, the U.S. penal system is horrendously costly. Since 1980 it has grown by 4.5 fold and totals 2.2 million incarcerated people—higher per the total population than any other OECD country and four times the world average. The usual figure cited for incarcerating criminals is $80 billion per year.

Some researchers, however, say the cost of jails and prisons is only one-tenth of the total "social cost" of crime, if that includes damage done to families and communities. The "overall" costs the data show amount to six percent of the gross domestic product or over $1 trillion a year.

Related to this problem is America's substance abuse crisis. The opioid crisis has cost a reported $1 trillion since 2001 and is climbing. This does not include other illegal drugs.

The expense of illegal immigrants in the United States is another huge burden. It is estimated the expenditures by government (state, local and federal) each year totals more than $134 billion. Since the taxes they pay amount to less than $18 billion the shortfall is $116 billion a year.

This figure is no doubt low, as it does not count the secondary costs or future expenditures.

The costs of these items to China are markedly less. For example, China has 300,000 lawyers (which arguably may not be enough); but the United States has 1.34 million (which according to a host of measures is way too many). In fact, many analysts see lawyers in the United States as a pernicious form of corruption.

China has 1.7 million incarcerated people, just over half the United States even though China's population is more than four fold America's. The cost per inmate is much less in China; China spends $22,000 per prisoner annually. California spends $75,000. New York City spends over $150,000. Yet the recidivism rate in China is much lower.

The drug problem in China is small compared to the United States. Almost in unison citizens in China (as in most Asian countries) say that illegal drug peddlers should be executed and if you do not believe that you hate your children and grandchildren. Many in the U.S. consider selling drugs a non-violent crime and thus not serious.

The cost of illegal immigrants in China is miniscule. China has accepted more than a million refuges from Vietnam. They were found jobs. China has foreign workers; but since China is not a welfare state they have not become a burden to taxpayers. Currently only immigrants that have skills are admitted. The United States almost alone accepts immigrants indiscriminately.

The list goes on.

The United States used to have a trade surplus with China—when China was a socialist (or communist) country and America was a capitalist country. Now that is reversed (judging from the percentage of the economy that is in the public sector in each and the United States is controlled by self-serving politicians).

Looking at the variances between the United States and China from a different angle, but one that also explains why the United States is not competing, Wendy Wang of the Institute for Family Studies notes one big difference between the two countries is what she calls "the sequence": education, work, marriage, children.

This explains a lot. In the United States for millennials who marry before having children the probability of being in poverty (and usually dependent on social welfare and unproductive) is 60 percent higher; for those out of sequence on three items it is 90 percent more. Having children out of wedlock is the worst. In China less than 4 percent of children are born out of wedlock. In the United States it is 40 percent (70 plus percent for blacks).

The "social" and "extra" financial costs the United States bears mean its business sector is less competitive. These "charges" impede exports and to a large degree explain the trade deficit. Together with government welfare they stifle business and account for the trade deficit.

It is not helpful that many economists suggest the trade deficit and the growing debt are not intimately related. But they are. The trade deficit slows GDP growth and reduces tax revenues. Debt increases.

Managed trade may fix this. Free trade, which is given lip service to in the United States, will not; in fact, it makes it a permanent problem thanks to America's political class.

TWENTY-SIX

China Robs U.S. Intellectual Property and Technology

How True? How Big? How to Fix It?

At the G20 meeting held in Buenos Aires, Argentina from November 30 to December 1, 2018, President Donald Trump and President Xi Jinping met to discuss two serious problems that have caused rising tension between their two countries: China's role in the U.S. trade deficit and the loss of American intellectual property (IP) and technology.

The two presidents seemed sincere in dealing with the problems and restoring workable and friendly United States-China relations. Reporters said they declared a "cease fire" and will endeavor to work things out in a designated period of 90 days.

That timetable seems critical as at the end of the period China will convene its National People's Congress and President Trump will again apply tariffs that he put on hold if the two issues are not resolved.

President Xi promised to buy more U.S. products. He even offered a figure: More than a trillion dollars worth. He also pledged to cut tariffs on U.S. autos and other products to help reduce the U.S. trade deficit with China.

Since more specifics were cited about the trade deficit and actions were taken forthwith, the IP/technology issue seemed to be the big obstacle to overcome. Thus the U.S. imputations on this matter provoke questions that need answers.

Question 1: Is it true China is stealing American IP and technology? Almost all on the American side say yes, of course, it is. Bolstering that view, legal cases have been filed and charges answered. There have been indictments and even extraditions of some people deemed guilty.

President Xi has cited U.S. "reasonable concerns." In a speech in 2017 he declared there was a need to do something and subsequently said there would be a "heavy price" to pay for violators. He later mentioned 38 punishments and suggested China's controversial (in the West) social credit system would play a part. He has repeated this since the G20 meeting.

On the other hand, many other Chinese leaders and the Chinese media quite consistently deny the allegations. Both have a quite different perception of what is going on. Also there is a problem of definitions. Thus it is uncertain what will happen going forward.

In any case President Trump believes the theft charges are true. Furthermore, he has connected them to the U.S. trade deficit with China, the loss of American jobs and his promise to "make America great again." Not only is China getting U.S. technology in surreptitious ways, he says, it is making products derived from that and is selling them to U.S. consumers.

The issue has salience with Democrats who (and this is very unusual) agree with President Trump. Democratic Senate Leader Chuck Schumer said that he wasn't in sync with Trump on anything but does support his punitive tariffs on China. Other Democrat leaders made similar statements.

Thus some observers think the issue may soon reach a "critical mass" and will precipitate a trade war.

Question 2: What is the backdrop?

Nations have long pinched other countries' IP and technology—the United States included. In fact, the United States began more than two centuries ago purloining British know-how in building textile machinery, thereby threatening the U.K.'s biggest export industry while building one in the United States.

It grew from there. One of Alexander Hamilton's deputies even published a system of bounties to attract sellers of trade secrets. At nearly the same time the United States. Congress passed a law to restrict registering patents in the United States to American citizens in order to shield the United States from this practice.

Anyway Americans went on to grab much more than blueprints to build a better textile machine. Basic research, patents, production techniques and much more became targets. This went so far that foreign technology became a boon to the American industrial revolution and to a fast growing U.S. economy in the nineteenth century and beyond.

During World War II American attitudes, and policies, about embezzling others' technology made a *volte-face*. The idea that technology should be free flowing, which many scientists and globalists of the time advocated, was nixed. It had to be protected. The case most cited was the work on the atomic bomb. The United States didn't want others to obtain this fearsome weapon.

After the war the practice of classifying weapons research was kept intact. The Cold War provided the justification. Further, this policy was extended into other areas than those related to weapons development.

Meanwhile the United States became the world's leader in almost all realms of scientific research. Americans didn't look abroad much to steal technology. Rather they had to fret about others stealing theirs.

However, except for weapons research, for some time America losing its IP and technology to others was not a big deal since the United States was able to keep ahead of all competitors. Also it didn't matter when it involved small countries that did not challenge America's world power status. So, a host of countries were allowed to poach American technology.

But recently it has become a serious matter because of the realization this affects the trade balance, American jobs and the U.S. debt. Equally important America's high tech losses, not just in military technology, are now linked to the contest for world power status.

In the past China didn't enter the discussions. But that changed; in fact, China has become a challenge of a different order. It is now the world's foremost economic power if that is measured by purchasing power or if one considers its number one ranking in the world in manufacturing and trade.

The question then arose: Should China be singled out for condemnation simply because of its size? That is unfair, isn't it? No, said most U.S. observers. When global power status is at stake the world is not fair.

Hence China's "Made in China 2025" project announced in 2015, after a short delay became a kind of "Sputnik moment" for the United States. China's leaders envisioned China becoming the world's leader in high tech manufacturing, advanced research and much more and it set forth plans to accomplish this, including getting new technology wherever and however it could (though it had been doing this for some time).

America reacted. In 2017 the Pentagon warned that state-led Chinese investment in U.S. firms working on facial recognition, 3-D printing, virtual reality systems and more blurred the lines between civilian and military technologies and was a danger to America. U.S. intelligence agencies subsequently declared China's theft of intellectual property and its targeting certain U.S. firms for acquisition was an "existential threat."

Question 3: How much does China's seizing American intellectual property and technology cost the United States?

According to President Trump it amounts to hundreds of billions of dollars. Due to its magnitude as well as its now perceived serious negative impact on the U.S. economy, Trump linked it to the trade deficit problem. Thus in March he threatened to put tariffs on at least $50 billion of Chinese imports into the United States and then did so. He subsequently added $200 billion and said there was another $267 billion "to go."

The Commission on the Theft of American Intellectual Property confirmed President Trump's estimates, reporting that the losses to the United States were between $180 billion and $540 billion per year, adding that "China accounts for most of that." But the gap between the low number and high figure was big and wording "most of that" was vague.

The United States Trade Representative then stated that "Chinese theft of American IP" costs between $225 and 600 billion annually. Again the span of the figures was big and it was not clear why this has happened or who pays these costs.

Anyway these numbers are much larger than previous estimates. In 2011 the U.S. Trade Commission reported that in 2009 U.S. firms lost $48 billion due to "Chinese infringements." Apparently President Obama and previous presidents did not want to draw attention to the issue and this explains the discrepancy. Or China's acquisitions grew at almost warp speed.

Question 4: What exactly is China doing?

The Chinese government requires foreign companies, such as those that have new energy vehicle technology, to share it. It also puts contractual restrictions on many foreign companies with business connections in China.

China obtains U.S. technology through cyber intrusions into U.S. government and private company computers, in other words via hacking. State-owned companies, private firms, and individuals all do this. The proportion of each, though, is not clear.

China has and uses many other ways to acquire U.S. know-how. Buying U.S. companies is one of them.

Yet much of China obtaining U.S. IP and technology comes from simply going through published articles or other information that can be found in libraries and online. America's freedom of the press and its generally free flow of research data abet China's efforts.

Also helping China are 100,000 Chinese students (mostly in the sciences) studying in the United State. They learn from taking courses and working in the United States after they graduate. If they return to China they often work for Chinese firms or the government that seek new IP and technology.

Last but far from the least, a whole lot of China getting technology it wants comes from Chinese companies' deals with American companies whereby the latter relinquish their trade secrets in return for access to China's huge (the largest in the world) market. This is done through simple negotiations, taking advantage of American companies' desire for large short-term profits.

Question 5: What are the cures? And what aren't?

First, what are not good remedies? Cutting the number of Chinese students in the United States is not a good idea. Their presence advertises the quality of American education and the advantages of the U.S. free market system, while they enrich the learning experience of other students. They also help the U.S. balance of payments.

The United States should not cut the number of joint ventures or China investing in U.S. companies, except when these companies have contracts with the government that involve defense secrets. Joint ventures and foreign investment bring ideas and technology to the United States and improve U.S. companies. On the other hand some new restrictions are certainly in order and the process must be made to work both ways.

President Trump should pressure U.S. companies not to give away their technology in return for access to the Chinese market. It will be difficult to stop this given the relationship between government and companies in the United States. But making issue of it may reduce it.

The Trump administration must take measures to counter cyber attacks and hacking, no matter where this comes from and whether or not a government is involved. It is hard to discern if technology theft comes from an individual hacker or whether a foreign intelligence service is involved and often what countries are guilty. Anyway a much higher level of vigilance is needed, as are more severe punishments.

President Trump needs to treat the loss of American IP and technology to China as a part of the imbalance of trade issue and persuade and/or pressure China to change its policies so that American does not suffer from either a trade or technology deficit relationship. The reality is it is difficult to measure the scope or value of technology losses, or who exactly is responsible; thus it will simplify matters to lump the problem of technology theft and the trade deficit together.

The president has to also ensure the animus toward China espoused by the mainstream media, Hollywood and academe in the United States, which all hate China intensely (because it threatens the liberal world order and embarrasses the United States' political left with charges of racism in college and university admissions) does not result in their gaining undue influence over United States-China negotiations.

Question 6: Recommendations?

Negotiations can and should solve the two problems. Donald Trump is a transactional president. China has suffered as a result of the disputes and seems willing to make a broad, or combined, deal. They can and need to negotiate.

The United States should prepare to steal (or otherwise acquire) Chinese IP and technology. China is now the leading nation in the world in registering patents and producing scientific papers. It is putting vastly more money into research in robotics, quantum computers, and artificial intelligence, three of the world's most cutting-edge technologies and three realms that will decide future national power capabilities.

Former Secretary of the Treasury Larry Summers advises that most of China's recent breakthroughs in technology are not the result of theft from the United States, but rather stem from China's "huge investments in basic science and terrific entrepreneurs."

If that doesn't characterize the U.S. dispute with China currently over U.S. IP and technology losses, it soon will. In other words, the question will soon see the shoe on the other foot.

Finally, the United States and China must realize resolving America's technology losses and the trade dispute with China are a *sine qua non* to better United States-China relations and are essential to keep the global financial system stable, resolve the problem of nuclear proliferation, deal with the international environment, check terrorism and much more. Thus successful negotiations are critical to resolve the two problems at hand.

TWENTY-SEVEN

America and China

Long-Term Friends or Enemies?

Since the beginning of Donald Trump's presidency relations between the United States and China have witnessed extremes of friendliness and cordiality on the one hand and hostility and antagonisms on the other hand. The recently coined term "frenemy" describes the relationship.

In 2018, especially toward the middle of the year, United States-China relations turned hostile over the issues of the U.S. trade deficit with China and China's alleged pinching U.S. intellectual property and technology. Some observers opined this situation would worsen and would lead to permanent alienation and even war.

In counterpoint, these two problems seem likely to be resolved and the tension between the United States and China reduced immeasurably. The United States and China will become cordial again and their relationship will be a working one to the benefit of both.

Which is it?

The key question that needs to be asked and answered is: What are the long-term trends relevant to the two countries being friends or foes? One must look at national power drifts, especially the ingredients of power and influence, to predict how America and China will get along, or not, in the future and how that will affect them and the international system.

One thing that is immediately clear is that the two, the United States and China, are the dominant world powers and that will be even more true in the future. Nobody else is seriously in the game.

How so? By almost all of the metrics used to gauge world power status, the bloc or nations competing with the United States and China, namely the European Union, Japan and Russia, are falling behind. Moreover, there is little hope any of the three will be able to reverse this trend.

Economic growth as measured by the gross domestic product (GDP) of a bloc or nation is the most commonly cited criteria for anticipating future world power rankings. The *Economist* predicts Western Europe's growth in 2019 to be 1.7 percent. (Germany, which is said to be the dynamo of Europe's growth) will see a 1.8 percent increase. Japan is forecast to record only 1.4 percent growth. Russia will see 1.8 percent expansion.

The United States, which owns the world's largest economy, is expected to grow at a rate of 2.2 percent. China is second in economic size. Its growth is projected to be 6.2 percent, more than three fold the world power wannabes.

Perceptions also matter. According to a World Bank survey (in 2017) 42 percent of people in the world see the United States as the world's top economic power while 32 percent opine it is China. Only 9 percent think it is the European Union and 7 percent view it as Japan.

Looking ahead, the International Monetary Fund projects China will have the planet's largest economy in 2030. The United States will be number 2. Japan will be number 4. Russia will be number 7; Germany will be 8. Projecting further into the future, in 2050, China will be number 1 by a bigger margin, Japan will be number 7, Russia will be 8th, Germany will rank 10.

According to *Defense News,* in security spending, the usual way of measuring a nation's military strength, the United States leads others by a big margin, double Europe. China is the second largest. Russia is roughly one-tenth the United States and below Saudi Arabia. Japan is around one-fifteenth the United States.

Says *Statista,* funding for research and development, another important metric of global power, the United States and China together account for half of the world's spending. China budgets two and a half times Japan and four times Germany for R&D. The European Union lags both the United States and China though not too far; however, its increases are only around 2 percent, below the United States, Russia and Japan's increases and far lower than China's, which is in the range of 17 to 18 percent.

In spending on research that is critical to future national power, especially in areas such as artificial intelligence and quantum computers, China leads. The United States is second. Others are way behind.

The United States and China own all of the large, top twenty, Internet companies. (11 are in the America, 9 are in China.)

Land, population, political systems and diplomacy, that were traditional measures of national power, are not seeing any meaningful trends. The United States and China are the largest countries in the world in terms of land area in a climate zone where human activity is meaningful, though Russia and Canada are bigger. In population China is first in the world; the United States, following India, is third. There is some discussion about the current failings of democratic systems and the Beijing "consensus" winning the race; but it seems too early to arrive at conclusions about this since governance is changeable.

Taking cognizance of the above it seems clear the global system is dominated by two powers. In other words it is a bipolar one.

The question then is: Which power, the United States or China will be the stronger, or the predominant one, in the future? They are and will be in the future competing with each other for global power status.

One can best formulate an answer to this question by examining at the advantages and disadvantages each has vis-à-vis the other and trends therein.

First, China's assets or advantages.

China has much larger financial assets than the United States measured in foreign exchange on hand—three plus trillion dollars (not counting huge individual and family savings). The United States has a debt approaching 22 trillion dollars. Over 6 trillion is owned to foreigners, China being the largest holder.

China's large financial holdings means it will gain further sway over global institutions and increase its control over the global financial system as a whole. It means China can provide more foreign aid and investments to other countries and thus influence developing countries. As I detail in my recent three-volume book on the subject, entitled *China's Foreign Aid and Foreign Investment Diplomacy,* China is fast doing both.

China has recently become the world's largest nation in manufacturing and trade. Both give China a leg up in global economic influence. Also, China continues to grow in both realms.

Having money also enables China to fund increasingly larger defense budgets and obtain more modern weapons. Likewise, it is able to pay for more scientific research and translate research into new products and thereby sustain a favorable trade balance.

China can also afford to send its students abroad to America's and Europe's best and most expensive colleges and universities. Its students in the United States number more than 350,000 or around one-third of the total foreign student population in America. Furthermore, most are studying engineering and the hard sciences, which analysts of national power say contributes more than students studying social sciences and the humanities that are the majority in the United States.

Chinese nationalism, which is largely a reaction to China's "century of humiliation" at the hands of the West and its citizens' desire to excel in response to this, enable its leaders use to win support for their strategies to improve China's power status in the world. This is an advantage to China in competing with the United States.

Chinese even say that the racial discrimination they face in the United States when their students apply for admission to America's best colleges and universities, the race bias practiced by Hollywood in making T.V.

shows and movies, and the liberal Western media castigating China and Chinese makes them more driven to work hard and succeed.

What are America's advantages?

The U.S. economy, measured in absolute terms, is the largest in the world. It is almost half again China's nominal gross domestic product. According to the *Wall Street Journal*, GDP per capita in the United States is $62,000 annually, compared to China's just over $10,000. This means that the United States does not need to grow as fast as China since its population is already rich and China's is not and China must sustain higher growth rates to keep its citizens happy.

The United States is growing faster than other developed countries. America can thus afford to spend more on defense (and does) and R&D. Further, since its currency is the main international tender it can extend aid and credits simply by printing more dollars. Other nations cannot do this.

Arguably the largest asset the United States possesses vis-à-vis China is the fact it has allies throughout the world that would help America in the event of a power struggle with China or in case of a war. The United States has military alliances and bases throughout the planet (800 in 70 countries according to *Politico* magazine). The U.K., France and Russia combined have bases in 30 countries. China has very few, perhaps not even one that is meaningful.

Projected increases in America's defense spending under President Trump are also bigger than China's. America's military training is better and its armed forces have been at war recently and thus are more seasoned fighters than China's (which have not been involved in conflict for some time).

Thus the military power balance between the United States and China favors America by a significant margin. Most experts believe this will not change for ten years or perhaps much longer. China's leaders have confirmed this.

Another realm where the United States excels, even dominates, is in soft power, which Joseph Nye, Jr. defines in his book *Soft Power: The Means to Success in World Politics,* as the "ability to get what one wants through attraction rather than coercion or payments."

America exerts global influence through its prominent role in films, music, fashion, music, the arts, sports, the media and promoting the English language. All of these contribute to America's soft power that far exceeds that of other countries. China is but number 21 in a *U.S. News and World Report* list of countries ranked by soft power.

America's influence in the media is especially strong. Its companies constitute the three largest in the world: Alphabet (Google), Comcast and Disney. America has 8 of the 10 largest (the non-U.S. two are in Japan and Holland).

The United States and China also face distinct disadvantages in dealing with the other.

China's economy is in the unenviable position of being sandwiched cum squeezed between countries that are more developed and have a higher level of technology and productivity and less developed countries that have considerably cheaper labor. China has coped well so far; but that cannot be ensured in the future.

President Trump imposing tariffs on China's imports has hurt China's economy seriously. Exports have dropped. Its stock market has fallen. Citizens' confidence has been affected adversely. Future growth seems uncertain. Certain companies, including some of China's biggest and best, have suffered.

Chinese politics have become less stable. Political (and social) tranquility as well as the Chinese Communist Party's credibility depends on continued good GDP growth and that is now being questioned.

For the United States its financial situation, especially its large debt, creates serious worry. Continually increasing its debt is patently unsustainable. Yet the problem continues to get worse. America's financial problems suggest a dim future.

The costs of its legal system, crime, welfare and illegal immigration are very burdensome and are getting worse. This makes the interest on the national debt a heavy weight on the economy and the society. Soon America will not be able to afford its defense spending or devote more money to R&D.

America is badly divided politically and decision-making is dysfunctional. Many feel the system is unfair; some say it is in a state of collapse.

Looking at the advantages and disadvantages the United States and China have vis-à-vis the other suggests their contest for power is quite asymmetric. This means they can cooperate on many fronts without competition becoming a source of conflict.

Even more poignant, Henry Paulson, former secretary of the treasury and author of *Dealing with China: An Insider Unmasks the New Economic Superpower,* says their need to cooperate to make the international system work is compelling. In other words, their relationship is "too big to fail."

One may conclude that the two-pole system made up of a powerful United States and a robust China, the two being far ahead of other powers, or bipolarity, worked during the Cold War; out of control conflict did not occur. Arguably it is a better system than a multipolar one, notwithstanding the fact many in the Western media and a host of national leaders favor multipolarity. Top international relations theorists such as Kenneth Waltz (author of *The Theory of International Politics)* and many other realist thinkers say multipolarity is the least stable system while bipolarity is the most stable. Unipolarity, of the immediate post-Cold War days, of course, has few supporters.

Index

academe, 84, 91, 93, 135
Afghanistan war, Donald Trump's actions in, 54
Africa: as fast growing region, 82; foreign aid and investments from China, 31, 113
AIIB,. *See* Asian Infrastructure Investment Bank
air pollution, 83
Allison, Graham, 84, 99
America. *See* United States
American Chamber of Commerce China survey, 77
anticnn.com website, 83
anti-Trump prejudice. *See* Western media
APEC Economic Leaders' Meeting, 60
The Art of the Deal (Trump), 2, 122
The Art of War (Sun Tzu), 1, 2, 40, 47, 121
Asahi Shimbun, on 2017 Asia trip, 59
Ash Center for Democratic Governance and Innovation (Harvard University), 107
Asia-Africa Growth Corridor (AAGC), 49
Asian Development Bank, 12, 48, 53
Asian Infrastructure Investment Bank (AIIB), 12, 22, 30, 32, 48
Asian media, on 2017 Asia trip, 58–60, 81
Asian pivot. *See* pivot to Asia
Asia trip, 2017, 57
Associated Press: on 2017 Asia trip, 58; on reciprocal tariffs, 87
Association of Southeast Asian Nations, 32
The Atlantic, on trade wars, 88

Baidu facial recognition, 105
Bangkok Declaration, 122
Bangladesh, support for BRI, 50
Bannon, Steven Kevin, 51–52, 54, 55, 100
Beijing consensus, 66
Belt and Road Initiative (BRI): Donald Trump's support for, 4, 53; financial resources for, 9, 114; global influence of, 82; human rights and, 49, 53; Obama on, 22; opponents and detractors, 48–49; as part of China Dream, 107; projected benefits, 50; as "Project of the Century", 30, 47–48; support for, 49–50; Western media on, 122
bipolar world system, 39, 139, 141
Boeing Company, 77
Bohai Strait tunnel, 31
Bolton, John, 117
Breitbart, 55
Brexit, 80
BRI. *See* Belt and Road Initiative
Burma, BRI, support for, 50
Bush, George H. W., 21, 65, 78
Bush, George W., 11, 65, 78, 111

Carter, Jimmy, 21, 65
Central China Television, 17
Chiang Kai-shek, 21, 123
China: Afghanistan war and, 54; air pollution, 83; anti-Western nationalism, 21; artificial intelligence, leadership in, 105, 109, 115; assets as world power, 139; Bannon on, 51, 52; bipolarity with U.S., 25, 27; candidate Trump on, 1; China Dream, 26, 47, 107, 112, 118, 122; Chinese Civil War, 21; citizen participation in politics, 83; convergence factor, 102;

cooperation with U.S., advantages of, 141; Countering Disinformation and Propaganda Act of 2017, 17; criminal justice and penal expenses, 73, 129; currency valuation, 70, 88, 126; cyber-warfare and cyber defense, 117; debt imbalance with U.S., 10; disadvantages dealing with U.S., 141; domestic issues, 24; Donald Trump, skepticism of, 22; Donald Trump on one-China policy, 23–24; as East Asia leader, 112; as Eastern/Western polarizing factor, 48; economic growth vs. U.S., 11; Europe's influence on military, 25; foreign aid and investments, 9, 29, 30–31, 82, 113; foreign currency exchange, 108; free market economy under Deng, 113; government on Donald Trump, 19; green energy in, 66, 114; Hollywood interests, 17; humiliation by West, 109; illegal immigrants, 73, 129; increasing exports from U.S., 127; innovative character, 106; intelligence against U.S., 118; international trade relations, 83; internet on 2017 Asia trip, 60; as largest trading nation, 29; legal expenses, 73, 129; Made in China 2025, 133; manned submersible crafts, 105; media on Donald Trump, 19–20; media presence in U.S., 17; as meritocracy, 108; middle class growth, 9; nationalism of, 139; networking strength, 109–110; non-interference principle, 118–119; North Korea, foreign aid to, 43–44; North Korea, punitive actions toward, 44; North Korea, relationship with, 24, 25, 96, 97; North Korea, troops in, 42; North Korea oil embargo, 97; North Korea sanction results, 42, 95; North Korea threat and, 54; Pakistan, aid to, 30; patents, trademarks, and industrial design, 8; pivot to Asia and, 12; political instability, 141; population's view of Donald Trump, 117; pre-2008 economic growth, 10; prediction of collapse, 112; prediction of democracy in, 112; as protectionist, 70, 126; quantum physics, leadership in, 105, 109, 115; reality of relations with U.S., 35; research ability, 108–109, 114, 127; size and population, 112; from socialism to capitalism, 125, 129; solar energy development, 32; space exploration vs. U.S., 8; status as world power, 7, 8; student exchange with U.S., 66, 134, 139; students in hard sciences and computers, 117; substance abuse problem, 73, 129; tariffs' effect on economy, 141; technology investment, 133; tensions with U.S., viii; Tianhe-1A computer, 8, 105; in Tibet, 83; trade balance with U.S., 19; 2008 recession, economy during, 106; U.S., friendship and hostility to, 63, 137; U.S., investments in, 1, 126, 134, 135; U.S., war possibility with, 40, 84, 99–100, 101, 102; U.S. debt growth to, 126; U.S. election interference, 117, 118; U.S. elections, effects on, 64–66; U.S. history, students of, 20–21; vs. U.S. involvement, 31; as U.S.'s greatest challenger, 112; U.S. tariff effects, 64; Western media's views of, 82; world GDP and, 9; WTO membership results, 88–89. *See also* Belt and Road Initiative (BRI); human rights; intellectual property theft; military power, China; poverty reduction by China,

China Daily, on 2017 Asia trip, 59

China Dream, 26, 47, 107, 118, 122

China Global Television Network, 17

China's Foreign Aid and Foreign Investment Diplomacy (Copper), 139

China's Megatrends (Naisbitt), 109

Chinese American discrimination, 122–123

Chinese Americans on Donald Trump, 124

Chinese investments in America, 1, 126, 134, 135

Chosun Ilbo, on 2017 Asia trip, 59
Chu, Steven, 8
Clinton, Bill: China, relationship with, 78; on China and WTO, 89; China effects on U.S. presidency, 65; debt imbalance with China, 11; on human rights in China, 65, 78; lack of respect for as president, 111
Clinton, Hillary, 7, 22, 61
CNBC, on 2017 Asia trip, 58
CNN: on 2017 Asia trip, 58; on reciprocal tariffs, 87
Cold War, 101
Commission on the Theft of American Intellectual Property, 134
convergence factor, 102
Conway, Kellyanne, 80
Copper, John, 139
Countering Disinformation and Propaganda Act of 2017, 16–17
criminal justice and penal expenses, 72, 73
Cuba, human rights abuses, 91
currency devaluations, 126
currency wars, 70, 76
cyber attacks, 134, 135
cyber-warfare, 21, 117, 119

Dalian Wanda Group, 17
Dealing with China (Paulson), 4, 102, 141
debt imbalance with China, 10, 70, 71
Defense News, on defense spending, 138
Delano, Warren, 123
democracy, declining support for, 113
Democratic Party: China election issues, 66, 67; intellectual property theft, 132; mid-term elections, 78
Deng Xiaoping, 25, 106, 108, 112, 113
Destined for War (Allison), 84, 99
Diamond, Jared, 106
Dick Clark Productions, 17
dollar as international currency, 140
Dunford, Joseph, Jr., 44
Duterte, Rodrigo, 60

East China Sea, 21
e-commerce, 8
Economist: on 2017 Asia trip, 58; on Western Europe's growth, 138
Espionage Act of 1917, 80
Europe: on BRI, 48–49; domestic issues, 39
European Union, 49, 137

Fairbanks, John, 106
fake news, 84
Ferguson, Niall, 26
Financial Times, on reciprocal tariffs, 87
foreign aid and investment,. *See under* China
foreign policy legacy, 7
Forum on China-Africa Cooperation, 32
Freedom of Information Act of 1967, 80
Freeman, Charles, 21
free trade issues, 70, 73, 126

G20 meeting, 131
Geneva Convention of 1925, 34
Gingrich, Newt, 3
global economic crisis of 2008–2009, 10
Global Times: on 2017 Asia trip, 59; huanqiu.com survey on Donald Trump, 19
Goldsmith, James, 113
The Governance of China (Xi), 25, 107
Greenspan, Alan, 125
gross domestic product (GDP), 138
Guo Wengui, 117

Haass, Richard, 2, 25, 100, 101
hacking and cyber attacks, 134, 135
Halleyman, Robert, 88
Harvard University, 122–123
Hayden, Michael, 21
Hearst, William Randolph, 91
Herman, Arthur, 109
Hollywood interests, 84, 91, 93, 135
huanqiu.com survey on Donald Trump, 19
Hu Jintao, 106
human rights: B. Clinton on in China, 65, 78; BRI as threatening to, 4, 49; Donald Trump ignored in China relationship, 20, 35, 38; Europe on, 53; H. Clinton on in China, 22;

Obama on, 65; *Time* magazine on, 58; in Vietnam, 60; *Washington Post on*, 57; Western media on, 45, 83, 93, 113, 119, 122
The Hundred Year Marathon (Pillsbury), 124

illegal immigrants, 72, 73
import/export rates, 76
India: Belt and Road Initiative (BRI), 4; China, fear of, 49; domestic issues, 39
The Influence of Sea Power upon History (Mahan), 38
intellectual property theft: China's success at, 70–71, 127; from China to U.S., 135; from foreign enterprises, 70; G20 Xi/Donald Trump meeting on, 131–132; trade balance, effect on, 133–134, 135, 136; U.S. history of, 132; violation of rules charged, 75
International Monetary Fund, 32, 48, 53, 138
Internet development, 138
Internet political interference, 117

Jackson, Andrew, 26
Japan: on BRI, 4, 50, 53; China, fear of, 49; competition with U.S. and China, 137; domestic issues, 39
Japan Times, on 2017 Asia trip, 58
Jiang Zemin, 65, 106
Johnson, Lyndon B., 21
Joongang Ilbo, on 2017 Asia trip, 59

Kaplan, Morton, 39
Kelly, John, 52
Kennedy, John F., 21
Kennedy School, 107
Kim Jong-un, 42, 59, 96–97
Kissinger, Henry: *On China*, 121; Donald Trump conference with, 1, 2; U.S.-China relations, 21, 24–25, 53; *World Order*, 25; to Xi on Donald Trump, 34, 102
Korean unification, 96, 97
Kra Canal, 12, 31
Kuttner, Robert, 52

Lane, Rowanne Brewer, 80
Latin America, foreign aid and investments from China, 31
League of Nations, 21
Liaoning (Chinese aircraft carrier), 94
Lincoln, Abraham, 26
Liu He, 77
Luce, Edward, 100, 101

Macao, money laundering in, 44
"Made in China 2025" strategy, 63, 64, 133
Mahan, Alfred, 38
Mao Zedong, 21
Mar-a-Lago meeting,. *See* Xi/Trump Mar-a-Lago meeting
Maritime Silk Road. *See* Belt and Road Initiative (BRI)
Marshall Plan, 9, 30, 107, 114
Maximum Pressure Campaign (Vietnam), 60
McKinley, William, 26
Megatrends (Naisbitt), 109
Mekong River project, 31
military power, China: Chinese leadership on, 39, 54; as increasing, 49, 92, 113; secret weaponry, 8; uneven arms races, 100; Western media on, 61, 83
military power, U.S.: Afghanistan war, 54, 65; alliances and overseas bases, 140; in Asia, 54; vs. China, 140; China-U.S. communications re North Korea, 44–45, 54; collaboration with China, 27; defense spending, 38, 39, 81, 94, 100, 101, 140; Donald Trump's Asian policy, 54, 60; as important to Donald Trump, 3; measurement criteria, 138; under Obama, 12; pivot to Asia and, 32; in South Korea, 43; Sun Tzu on, 40; technology in, 133; as threat, 37, 38, 97; training, 140; uneven arms races and war, 100, 101; in various countries, 112; zero-sum theory, 89
Mnuchin, Steven, 76
Modi, Narendra, 49

Mongolia, foreign aid and investments from China, 31
Moon Jae-in, 59
Mueller investigation, 15, 81, 97
Mutual Assured Destruction, 40

Naisbitt, John, 109
National Defense Strategy report, 118
national power measures, traditional, 138
National Security Council, 51
Navarro, Peter, 100
NBC news: on 2017 Asia trip, 58; on BRI, 48
Needham, Joseph, 106
new world order, 25
New York Times: on 2017 Asia trip, 58; on BRI, 48; on Donald Trump's foreign policy experience, 1; on reciprocal tariffs, 87
Nixon, Richard, 21, 26, 123
North China Sea, 31
North Korea: Bannon on, 52; as buffer between China and U.S. forces, 43; China, relationship with, 24, 25, 41–42, 96; China actions against, 44, 45; China's help with, 34; China's views on, 42; China trade dispute link, 54; criminal activities, 96; foreign aid and investments from China, 96; as isolated from world, 43; nuclear testing and China, 44, 63, 76–77, 95, 96; oil embargo by China, 97; sanctions against, 42, 96, 97
Nye, Joseph, Jr., 140

Obama, Barack: Asian Infrastructure Investment Bank, 12, 22, 32, 48; Belt and Road Initiative (BRI), 4, 12, 22, 25, 48, 53; China, legislative moves re, 15; China, relationship with, 11, 21, 24, 85; China effects on presidency, 65; China/Taiwan policy, 16; Countering Disinformation and Propaganda Act of 2017, 16–17; debt imbalance with China, 10, 11; Donald Trump's Russian friendship and, 15; foreign policy legacy, 7; human rights in China, 65; international policies, 12, 16; Kra Canal, 12; leading from behind policy, 111; pivot to Asia, 7, 32; sequestration, 100; transnational, globalist presidency, 2; Trans-Pacific Partnership, 32; Western media on, 80; on Yuan as global currency, 12, 22, 32
OBOR. *See* Belt and Road Initiative (BRI)
On China (Kissinger), 121
one-China policy, 23–24
100-days of negotiations plan, 3–4
One Road One Belt (OBOR) plan. *See* Belt and Road Initiative (BRI)
Opium War, 123
Organization for Economic Development and Cooperation, 12

Pakistan: BRI, support for, 50; China's aid to, 30; economic and political position, 30; foreign aid and investments from China, 54
Paulson, Henry, 4, 53, 102, 141
The Peloponnesian War (Thucydides), 99
Pew Foundation, 12, 83, 108
Philippines: China vs. U.S. involvement, 31; on 2017 Asia trip, 60
Philippine Star, on 2017 Asia trip, 60
Pillsbury, Michael, 124
pivot to Asia, 7, 11, 12, 20, 22, 32, 48
Politico, on U.S. allies, 140
Pope Francis, 2, 84
Pottinger, Matt, 49
poverty reduction by China, 9, 49, 66, 82, 106, 113, 129
Priebus, Reince, 52
Pulitzer, Joseph, 91
Putin, Vladimir, 15, 49

Qinghua University, 108

racism against Asians: in colleges and universities, 135; Donald Trump's racism, 91; from liberals, 113; in U.S., 66; Western media, 109; Wilson known for, 20

Radio Voice (Vietnam), on 2017 Asia trip, 60
Reagan, Ronald, 21, 26, 65
realist political philosophy, 100
regulations' effects on trade deficit, 71
The Retreat of Western Liberalism (Luce), 100
Ricardo, David, 88
Rice, Susan, 58
Roosevelt, Franklin, 21, 26, 123
Roosevelt, Theodore, 26
Russia: competition with U.S. and China, 137; domestic issues, 39
Russian collusion investigation. *See* Mueller investigation

Schumer, Chuck, 58, 132
Science and Civilization in China (Needham), 106
Segal, Adam, 117
"the sequence", 73, 129
Shandong Province, 20
Shanghai Cooperation Organization, 32
Silk Road. *See* Belt and Road Initiative
Sina Weibo, 19
Soft Power (Nye, Jr.), 140
soft power, 140
solar energy development in China, 32, 75, 76
South China Sea, 21, 31, 34, 93
South Korea: U.S. forces in, 43; U.S. help with self-defense methods, 59
Soviet Union, China vs. U.S. involvement, 31
space exploration, 8
Spanish-American War, 91
Sri Lanka support for BRI, 50
Statista, on research ability, 138
stock market activity, 87
student exchanges, China and U.S., 66, 134, 139
Students for Fair Admission, 122–123
Stuxnet, 119
Summers, Larry, 135
Sun Tzu, 1, 2, 40, 47, 90, 121
#Super Tuesday, 19
Syria, missile strike on, 33, 34, 38
Taiwan: Obama's policy on, 16; Taiwan independence, 100; Taiwan trigger, 100, 102; U.S. military exercises with, 16
Taiwan Relations Act of 1979, 65
tariffs: candidate Trump on, 1; China, effects on, 118; from China, 64; China's intellectual property and technical theft cost and, 133; on Chinese goods, 118; imposed, 2018, 75; reciprocal tariffs, U.S. and China, 87
taxes, trade deficit effects on, 71
Taylor, Alexander, 113
technology, 70–71, 75
terrorism: Afghanistan as base for, 54; in China, viii; in North Korea, 42, 44; Pakistan's geographical position and, 30; U.S.-China relationship and, 27, 53, 102, 136
Thailand, foreign aid and investments from China, 31
The Theory of International Politics (Waltz), 141
Three Year Plan of Action for Defense Cooperation (Vietnam), 60
Thucydides, 99
Thucydides Trap, 35, 39, 99, 101
Tiananmen Square, 65
Tianhe-1A computer, 8, 105
Tibet, China's influence in, 83, 93
Tillerson, Rex, 43, 97
Time magazine, on 2017 Asia trip and human rights, 58
Time to Get Tough (Trump), 2, 3
tourism, 8
Trade Act of 1974, 52, 64
trade deficit: in *The Art of the Deal* , 122; Bannon on, 51; capitalism vs. socialism and, 113; causes, 89; China's intellectual property and technical theft cost and, 133, 135; Donald Trump's philosophies on, 88–89; effects of, 69; G20 Xi/Donald Trump meeting on, 131; Greenspan on, 125; hostility in China relations and, 63; size, 69; solutions, 71; U.S. debt growth and, 130; with various countries, 125; worsens in 2018, 75;

Xi/Trump Mar-a-Lago meeting, 53
trade imbalance with U.S.: agreements with China, 3, 34, 59, 118; Chinese leadership on, 67; currency devaluations for, 70; Donald Trump's support for BRI and, 25; free trade theory and, 88, 126; tariffs for, 75
trade surpluses, 69–70
trade war, 1, 24, 76, 87–88
Trans-Pacific Partnership, 11, 20, 32, 48, 58, 122
Treaty of Versailles, 20
Truman, Harry, 3, 21, 123
Trump, Donald: Afghanistan war, 54; on alliances, 38; *The Art of the Deal,* 2, 122; Bannon's dismissal, 51–52, 54; bipolar world view, 39; on BRI, 49, 101, 122; as candidate, 79–80; China, background on, 1–2; China, personal view of, 121, 122; China as biggest problem, vii; on China's intellectual property and technical theft cost, 133, 135; China's views on, 19–20, 124; China/Taiwan policy, 16; China trade dispute and North Korea link, 54; Chinese investors in America, 1; current world order, ending, 26; economic accomplishments, 81; foreign policy legacy from Obama, 7; free trade philosophy, 88; G20 meeting with Xi, 131; on global system, 25; grandchildren speaking Chinese, vii, 3, 121; human rights, 20, 35, 38; impeachment threats, 97; as isolationist, 38; military power in Asia, 54; Mueller investigation, 81; as nationalist, 2; negotiating with China, vii–viii, viii; on new world order, 25; on one-China policy, 23–24; political accomplishments, 81; pragmatism of, 124; as Russophile, 38; Silk Road, support for, 25; skepticism of in China, 22; social media use, 79; Syria, intervention in, 38; tariff effects on U.S. economy, 64; transactional presidency, 2; on Trans-Pacific Partnership, 20; 2017 budget agreement, 112; on United Nations, 39; views on chaos and mistakes, 3; at World Economic Forum, 76; world view of election, 111; worldview shift, 37–38, 40; Xi, relationship with, 3–4; Xi/Trump Mar-a-Lago meeting, 3, 33–36, 38, 53. *See also* Asia trip, 2017,
Trump Derangement Syndrome, 61
Trump Doctrine, 3, 37
Tsai Ing-wen, 23, 24
Twain, Mark, 94

Understanding Trump (Gingrich), 3
unemployment, 69
United Nations, 39, 113
United States: Asians, discrimination against, 113; assets as world power, 140; bipolarity with China, 25, 27; budget items, expensive, 71–72; on capitalism vs. socialism, 113; from capitalist to socialist, 125, 129; China, cooperation with, 141; China, disadvantages dealing with, 141; China, friendship and hostility to, 63, 137; China, increasing exports to, 127; China, reality of relations with, 35; China, tensions with, viii; China, trade balance with, 19; China, war possibility with, 40, 84, 99–100, 101, 102; classified weapons intelligence theft, 132–133; convergence factor, 102; corporate taxes and regulations, 127; criminal justice and penal expenses, 72, 128; debt growth, 125–126, 127, 130; debt imbalance with China, 10, 70, 71; dollar devaluation, 76; economy growth, 11, 76; health care costs, 127; illegal immigrants, 72, 128; import/export rates, 76; intellectual property theft, 132, 133; interest payment on debt, 69–70, 71, 72, 89, 126, 128, 141; legal expenses, 72, 128; manufacturing job decline, 125; middle class growth, 9; national debt, 89; North Korea, relationship with, 97; on North Korea's nuclear

sales, 43; one-China policy, 23–24; Pakistan, aid to, 30; political divisiveness, 141; pre-2008 economic growth, 10; social problems in, 114; social security, 127; space exploration vs. China, 8; student exchanges, China and U.S., 66, 134, 139; substance abuse problem, 72, 128; textile machinery plans theft, 132. *See also* military power, U.S.
unit-veto system, 39
U.S. allies, strength of, 140
USA Today, on 2017 Asia trip, 58
U.S. election interference by China, 117, 118
U.S. National Defense Authorization Act, 16
U.S. National Intelligence Council, 2
U.S. News and World Report: on most powerful country, 111; on soft power country ranking, 140
U.S. Trade Commission, 134

Vietnam: China vs. U.S. involvement, 31; human rights, 60

Wall Street Journal, on GDP comparison, 140
Waltz, Kenneth, 141
Wang, Wendy, 73, 129
Wang Jianlin, 17
Wang Qishan, 77
Washington Post: on 2017 Asia trip, 57; on Donald Trump and human rights, 57; on Donald Trump's foreign policy experience, 1
welfare state and U.S. debt, 125–126
Western media: on Asia, 61; on reciprocal tariffs, 87–88
Western media on China,: air pollution, 83; as authoritarian dictatorship, 82, 83, 122; on BRI, 4, 48, 53, 122; as cheating in trade, 126; dislike of, viii, 55, 61, 66, 79, 84, 89, 109, 113, 119, 135; on Donald Trump and China, 45, 81, 111–112; as economically successful, 82; Hollywood interests, 84; human rights in, 45, 83, 93, 113, 119, 122; intention of, 84; North Korea nuclear threat, 95; prediction of collapse, 93; in Tibet, 83; on trade issues, 70, 83; on Trump-Xi meeting, 33; as world power, 92; Xi as "whipping boy", 4
Western media on Trump: 2017 Asia trip, 57, 61, 62; as candidate, 79–80; on Donald Trump and China, 81; election year positions, 78; extensive complaints about, 91–92; Mueller investigation, 81; as president, 80–81; protectionism and isolationism of, 94; public trust in, 82; trade war created by, 76; Trump Derangement Syndrome, 61
Wilson, Woodrow, 20–21, 123
World Bank, 12, 48, 53, 138
World Economic Forum, 76
World Economic Union, 82
world Gross Domestic Product (GDP), 9
A World in Disarray (Haass), 2, 25, 100
World Order (Kissinger), 25
World Trade Organization (WTO), 70, 83, 88–89, 126

Xi Jinping: China Dream and innovations, 107; Donald Trump, relationship with, 3–4; Donald Trump on one-China policy, 23–24; on Donald Trump's tariffs, 90; G20 meeting with Donald Trump, 131; *The Governance of China* , 25, 107; new world order goal, 26; promoting China's rise, 112; ruling style, 83; summit meeting at Mar-a-Lago, 3, 33–36, 53; trade imbalance promises with U.S., 25, 77; T. Roosevelt comparison, 26; Western media on, 24, 81
Xi/Trump Mar-a-Lago meeting, 3, 33–36, 38, 53

Yalta, FDR's betrayal of China, 21
Yuan as global currency, 12, 22, 32, 114
Yugoslavia, NATO bombings, 119

About the Author

John Franklin Copper is the Stanley J. Buckman Distinguished Professor of International Studies (emeritus) at Rhodes College in Memphis, Tennessee. He is the author of more than 35 books on China, Taiwan, and U.S. China policy. His book *China's Global Role* (1980) won the Clarence Day Foundation Award for outstanding research and creative activity. Dr. Copper has also contributed to more than 40 other books and has published over 150 articles in scholarly journals, magazines, and newspapers.

Dr. Copper's recent books include the three volume work entitled *China's Foreign Aid and Foreign Investment Diplomacy* (2016), *Taiwan: Nation State or Province? sixth edition* (2013), *Taiwan at a Tipping Point* (2018).

Professor Copper has testified before several U.S. Congressional committees, including the Senate Foreign Relations Committee and the House Foreign Affairs Committee. In 1997 he was recipient of the International Communications Award for promoting global understanding. Dr. Copper has lived in Asia for 15 years.